OPENING STRATEGIES

STRATEGIES

AN INTEGRATED LANGUAGE COURSE FOR BEGINNERS OF ENGLISH

Brian Abbs
Ingrid Freebairn

Longman

Contents

Thistle Hotels

🎞 Dialogue: Part 1

WOMAN: Good morning.
DIANA: Good morning. My name's Diana Trent.

WOMAN: Ah, yes, Mrs Trent. Room 201. Here's your key.
DIANA: Thank you.

WOMAN: And what's your name, sir?
PAUL: Roberts.
WOMAN: Roberts. Are you Mr David Roberts?
PAUL: No, I'm not. I'm Paul Roberts.

Set 1 Names

1. My name's Diana Trent.
What's your name?

Ask and answer in pairs, like this:

A: My name's (Carlos). What's your name?
B: My name's (Juan).

2. What's his name? His name's Paul.
What's her name? Her name's Diana.

Look at the pictures above. Ask and answer about the people, like this:

What's his name? His name's Vince.

1. Vince Hall (Mr)   4. Diana Trent (Mrs)
2. Joanne Tessler (Miss)   5. Jack Feldman (Mr)
3. Paul Roberts (Mr)   6. Sally Jones (Miss)

3. Are you Paul Roberts? Yes, I am.
Are you David Roberts? No, I'm not. I'm Paul Roberts.

Look at the pictures again. Ask and answer, like this:

Are you Vince Hall? Yes, I am.

Ask these questions:

1. Are you Vince Hall?   4. Are you Diana Trent?
2. Are you Joanne Tessler?   5. Are you Bob Feldman?
3. Are you David Roberts?   6. Are you Nina Jones?

4. Is your name Paul Roberts? Yes, it is.
Is your name David Roberts? No, it isn't. It's Paul Roberts.

Ask and answer about the people in the pictures, like this:

1. Is your name Vince Hall? Yes, it is.

Use the names in the questions in Exercise 3.

5

Set 2 Greetings and titles

Good morning.

Good afternoon.

Good evening.

1.	Good morning, Mr Hall.

Greet the people throughout the day.

**Now greet a few people in your class. Use their first names.
Greet your teacher. Use his/her title.**

2. Look at the pictures below. Say Good morning,
Good afternoon, **or** Good evening.

3.	My name's Vince Hall. Good morning, Mr Hall.

Practise in the same way with the people on page 5.

📼 Dialogue: Part 2

WOMAN: Ah, yes. Here's your name.
Mr Paul Roberts.
Your room number is 202.

PAUL:　Thank you.
WOMAN: And here's your key,
Mr Roberts.
PAUL:　Thank you.

0	1	2	3	4	5	6	7	8	9	10
oh	one	two	three	four	five	six	seven	eight	nine	ten

1. Say these room numbers:

Room number	Name of Guest
201	Trent, D.
202	Roberts, P
305	Hall. V.
306	Tessler, J
708	Roberts. D
803	Jones, S
902	Feldman, J

2. Ask and answer with your partner, like this:

What's your telephone number?
It's 38994 (three, eight, double nine, four).

Then say the telephone numbers on the right.

3. Look at the international dialling codes for Australia and Austria.

Australia
CHARGE BAND 5B   Time difference between 8 and 10 hours later than GMT

International Code **010**	Country Code **61**	☆ Area Code	Subscriber's Number

Adelaide	8	Darwin	89	Newcastle	49
Albury	60	Dubbo	68	Orange	63
Ballarat	53	Geelong	52	Perth (W.A.)	9
Bathurst	63	Geraldton	99	Rockhampton	79
Brisbane	7	Hobart	02	Sydney	2
Bunbury	97	Kalgoorlie	90	Toowoomba	76
Bundaberg	71	Launceston	03	Townsville	77
Cairns	70	Melbourne	3	Wagga Wagga	69
Canberra	62	Mt. Gambier	87	Wollongong	42

Tones similar to those used in the UK.

Austria
CHARGE BAND 2   Time difference 1 hour later than GMT

International Code **010**	Country Code **43**	☆ Area Code	Subscriber's Number

Dornbirn	5572	Klagenfurt	4222	Steyr	7252
Gmunden	7612	Leoben	3842	Vienna	222
Graz	316	Linz, Donau	7222	Villach	4242
Innsbruck	5222	St. Pölten	2742	Wels	7242
Kitzbühel	5356	Salzburg	6222	Wiener Neustadt	2622

Tones: for a free demonstration of tones you may hear dial 100, ask for Freefone 2070

What is the complete number for:

Hans in Vienna — 23 44 03?   Bill in Melbourne — 856 7845?
Anna in Innsbruck — 77 89 043?   Katina in Sydney — 765 5322?

🔉 Open dialogue
You are in the Tower Hotel. Your room number is 401.
Talk to the hotel receptionist.

RECEPTIONIST: Good morning.
YOU: . . . .
RECEPTIONIST: Is your name Trent?
YOU: . . . .
RECEPTIONIST: Ah, yes. What's your room number?
YOU: . . . .
RECEPTIONIST: Thank you. Here's your key. Number 401.
YOU: . . . .

Roleplay
Work in groups of five or six. One of you is a hotel receptionist. The others are hotel guests. Make a list of people's names and give them each a room number. They arrive at the reception desk. Ask for their names. Give them room numbers and keys.

🔉 Listening
Listen to three guests arriving at a hotel. Fill in the missing name, number or title.

NAME	ROOM NUMBER
Mr Charles Roberts	503
Susan Jones	
Mr Churchill	

Reading

1.

Is your name John Porter?
No, it isn't.

2.

Are you John Porter?
No, I'm not. I'm Tim Webb.

3

John Porter?
No!

4.

Er. . . what's your name?
Charles Rider.
Oh.

5.

Are you Mr Porter?
Yes, I am. John Porter.

6

Oh good! I'm from The Tower
Language School. Welcome to
London.
Thanks.

Writing

1. Fill in this form for yourself:

Surname..	Mr/Mrs/Miss/Ms
First names..	
Address...	
Telephone number..	
Signed..	

2. Write a note to a friend, like this:

Dear Diana,
My address in London is
3 Carlton Gardens, London, W8
and my telephone number is
671 2113. Please write or phone.
Dave

Oral exercises

1. Introduce yourself
Good morning.
Good morning. My name's Vince Hall.

1. Vince Hall
2. Joanne Tessler
3. Paul Roberts
4. Diana Trent
5. Sally Jones
6. Jack Feldman

2. Confirm and correct information
Are you Paul Roberts?
Yes, I am.
Are you Diana Trent?
No, I'm not.

1. Paul Roberts/yes
2. Diana Trent/no
3. Jack Feldman/no
4. Sally Jones/yes
5. John Gibbs/yes
6. Sue Grant/no

3. Correct information
Is your name John?
No, it isn't. It's Jack.

1. John/Jack
2. Ann/Diana
3. Paul/David
4. Sally/Sue
5. Charles/Tim
6. Diana/Ann

4. Give people's names
What's his name?
His name's Paul.
What's her name?
Her name's Diana.

1. Paul
2. Diana
3. Tim
4. Joanne
5. Vince
6. Sue

5. Say numbers
My room number is 201.
Oh good! I'm in 202.

1. 201
2. 407
3. 508
4. 102
5. 206
6. 605

Grammar

What's (What is)	your his her	name?	My His Her	name's (name is)	Diana. Paul.

I'm It's	Paul Roberts.

Are you	Paul John	Roberts?	Yes, I am. No, I'm not.

Is your name	Paul? John?	Yes, it is. No, it isn't.

I'm (I am) You're (You are)	in room 204.

🔊 **Dialogue: Part 1**

DIANA: Hello. Are you here for the video conference?
VINCE: Yes, we are. Are you?
DIANA: Yes, I am.
VINCE: That's nice. I'm Vince and this is Joanne.
JOANNE: Hi. Pleased to meet you.

DIANA: Paul! Come and meet these people. Paul, this is Vince and Joanne. They're here for the conference, too.

PAUL: How do you do.
VINCE: That's neat! 'How do you do!' You British are very polite!

Answer yes or no.
Are Vince and Joanne in London for a conference?
Is Paul British?
Are Vince and Joanne British?

Set 1 Greetings and introductions

1. Hello. I'm Diana and this is Paul.
Hi. Pleased to meet you.

Work in groups of three. Use your own names like this:
Hello. I'm . . . and this is . . . .
Hi. Pleased to meet you.
Hello.

2. This is Mr Roberts.
How do you do.
How do you do.

Work in groups of three. Introduce these people formally:

Mr Hall   Mrs Trent   Miss Tessler   Mrs Feldman   Mr Roberts   Miss Jones

3. Excuse me. Is your name Paul Roberts?
Yes, it is.
Oh good! I'm Sally Jones. How do you do.
How do you do.

Work in pairs. Introduce yourselves to each other in the same way. Use your own names.

🔊 Dialogue: Part 2

DIANA: Where are you from?
VINCE: We're American.
We're from Los Angeles.
What about you two?
DIANA: We're from Manchester.

Set 2   Countries and nationalities

Frank and Lois from the USA

Sabine from France

Robert and Ann from Britain

Peter from Germany

Bruno and Sylvia from Italy

Ariadne from Greece

Juan from Mexico

Jorge from Brazil

Oumon from Senegal

Carlos from Spain

Habib from Egypt

Yoshimi from Japan

1. Hello. I'm Jorge. I'm from Brazil.
Hello. I'm Frank and this is Lois. We're from
the United States.

You are the other people. Introduce yourselves.

2. This is Yoshimi. She's from Japan.
This is Jorge. He's from Brazil.
This is Robert and Ann. They're from Britain.

Introduce the other people in the same way.

3. I'm from the United States. Where are you from?
I'm from Britain.

In pairs, introduce yourselves in the same way. Say where you are from.

4.

Brazil	Brazilian	Italy	Italian
Britain	British	Japan	Japanese
Egypt	Egyptian	Mexico	Mexican
France	French	Spain	Spanish
Germany	German	USA	American
Greece	Greek	Senegal	Senegalese

Use the names of the countries and the nationality words to identify each of the flags, like this: This is the British flag.

Then ask and answer about the flags, like this:
What's number 2?   It's the British flag.

5. Introduce yourselves, like this:
I'm (name) and I'm (nationality).

6. This is Jorge. He's Brazilian.
This is Sabine. She's French.
This is Bruno and Sylvia. They're Italian.

Introduce the other people on the map on page 14 in the same way.

7. Is Jorge Brazilian?   Is Sabine French?
Yes, he is.   Yes, she is.

Is Bruno Spanish?   Is Lois British?
No, he isn't.   No, she isn't.

Are Lois and Frank American?
Yes, they are.

Are Bruno and Sylvia Spanish?
No, they aren't.

Ask and answer about the people on the map:
1. Jorge/Spanish?
2. Robert and Ann/British?
3. Sabine/Italian?
4. Peter/German?
5. Yoshimi/Japanese?
6. Bruno and Sylvia/Mexican?
7. Habib/Spanish?
8. Carlos/Brazilian?
9. Juan/Spanish?
10. Oumon/British?

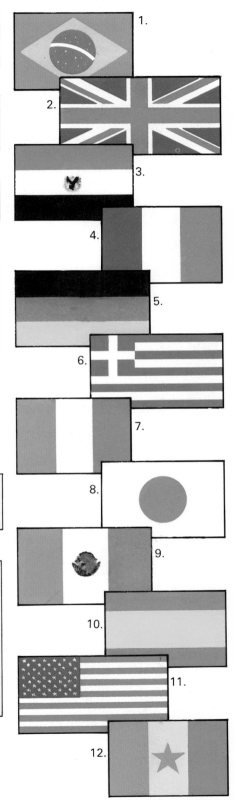

1.
2.
3.
4.
5.
6.
7.
8.
9.
10.
11.
12.

🔊 Dialogue: Part 3

DIANA: What's that, Paul?
PAUL: It's a map of London.
         Here's the Tower of
         London.
JOANNE: Oh yes. Where's Piccadilly
         Circus?
PAUL: It's over there.

MAN: Mr Hall?
VINCE: Yes?
MAN: Your taxi is here, Mr Hall.
VINCE: Thank you. Well, goodbye.
         Have a nice day!

Are these true or false?
Paul and Joanne are at
   the Tower of London.
Vince is in a taxi.

Set 3 Objects

1.
> What's that?
> It's a map of London.

Match the words in the box with each of the objects:

a key	a diary	an address book
a comb	a pen	an identity card
a wallet	a purse	an umbrella
a ticket	a pencil	

2. In pairs, identify each object, like this:
> What's that?
> It's a key.

3. Find three objects in your bag, purse or pocket. Hold them up and ask your partner to identify them, like this:
> What's this in English?
> It's a ticket.

4. In pairs, point to three things in the room and ask your partner to identify them, like this:
> What's that in English?
> It's an exercise book./It's a dictionary.

🔊 Open dialogue
Talk to Diana.

DIANA:	Hello.
YOU:	. . . .
DIANA:	What's your name?
YOU:	. . . .
DIANA:	I'm Diana. And this is a friend, Paul.
PAUL:	Hello.
YOU:	. . . .
DIANA:	We're British. We're from Manchester. Where are you from?
YOU:	. . . .
DIANA:	Well, enjoy your English class. Goodbye!
YOU:	. . . .

Roleplay

In groups of five. Choose to be one of these people:
Miss Josie Lewis from the USA
Robert and Ann Watkins from Britain
Mr Pierre Caron from France
Mrs Maria Contini from Italy
1. You are in a meeting. Introduce the other people formally.
   Use their titles and surnames.
2. You are at a party. Introduce the other people informally.
   Use their first names.

Start like this:

How do you do./Hello. My name's . . .. I'm from . . ..
This is . . .. He's (nationality).

🔘🔘 Listening

Listen to some people speaking. Write down which languages they
are speaking in the order you hear them.

Spanish	French	German
English	Japanese	

Reading

Hello. I'm Sylvana. I'm Italian. I'm from Milan. This is my class
at the Tower Language School. It's a small class, but it's nice.
We're all in Class 5. The students aren't all from Italy. They're
from Spain, France, Germany and Japan, too. My friend,
Sabine, is French. She's from Paris. She's a new student, but her
English is very good. Mr Lewis, the teacher, is from Manchester.
He's very nice and polite. He's a very good teacher, and we're very
good students!

Are these true or false?

Sylvana is Italian.
She's a teacher.
It's a big class.
Her friend is French.
All the students are from Italy.
Mr Lewis is an English teacher.
Mr Lewis is very nice.

Writing

1. Copy and fill in this form for yourself:

Surname...
First names..
Nationality ....
Place of birth...
Address...
Telephone number..

2. Write a paragraph about you and your class. Write like Sylvana.

Oral exercises

1. Meet people
Hello. I'm Jack.
Hello. Pleased to meet you, Jack.

1. Jack
2. Sue
3. Tim
4. Ann

2. Greet people formally
How do you do. My name's Vince Hall.
How do you do, Mr Hall.

1. Mr Vince Hall
2. Mrs Diana Trent
3. Miss Sally Jones
4. Mr Paul Roberts

3. Introduce people
I'm Jack and this is Ruth.

1. Jack and Ruth
2. Robert and Ann
3. Lois and Frank
4. Bruno and Sylvia
5. Diana and Paul
6. Joanne and Vince

4. Say where people are from
He's American. Where is she from?
She's from America, too.

1. American
2. British
3. French
4. Mexican
5. Italian
6. Greek

5. Say where you and your friends are from
Are you French?
Yes. We're from Paris.

1. French/Paris
2. Spanish/Madrid
3. American/New York
4. Japanese/Tokyo
5. Brazilian/Rio
6. Italian/Milan

Grammar

TO BE

This is	Paul. Joanne. the British flag.		

I'm (I am) You're (You are) He's (He is) She's (She is)	from	Milan. the States.
It's (It is) We're (We are) You're (You are) They're (They are)	Italian. American.	

Are you Is he Is she	from Britain?	Yes,	I am. he is. she is. it is. we are. they are.	No,
Is it Are you Are they	British?			I'm not. he isn't. she isn't. it isn't. we aren't. they aren't.

Where are you from?		I'm from the States.

What's	this? that?	It's	a map. an address book. the British flag.

Where's (Where is) my	taxi? book?

It's	here. over there.

Unit 3 | I like London

Dialogue: Part 1

PAUL: Oh hello, Joanne!
          How are you?
JOANNE: I'm fine thanks.
PAUL: Are you busy?
JOANNE: No.

PAUL: Let's have a cup of coffee.
JOANNE: OK. But not here in the
          hotel. Let's go out.

PAUL: Well, do you like London?
JOANNE: Yes, I do. Very much.
          I don't like Los Angeles
          very much, but I like
          London. It's a nice city.
PAUL: Yes, I like London, too.

20

Set 1   Greeting friends

Hello. How are you? I'm fine, thanks. And you? I'm very well, thank you.	Hi. How are you? Not too bad, thanks. And you? Fine, thanks.

Greet your teacher and your partner in the same way.

Set 2   Likes and dislikes (1)

1.	Do you like London?	Yes, I do. Yes, very much. No, I don't. No, not very much.

What do you like? Write your own answers, Yes or No.

		You	Your friend	Diana	Paul
Music:	Pop music Classical music			No Yes	Yes No
Animals:	Cats Dogs			Yes No	No No
People:	Children Babies			Yes Yes	Yes No

Now ask your partner, like this:
Do you like pop music?
Yes, I do./Yes, very much.
No, I don't./No, not very much.

Write down your partner's answers.

2.	I like pop music, but I don't like classical music. I like pop music and I like classical music, too. I don't like pop music or classical music.

Look at your answers to Exercise 1. Talk and write about your own likes and dislikes in the same way.

3.	Does Diana like classical music? Yes, she does. Does Paul like classical music? No, he doesn't.

Look at Diana's answers. Ask and answer, like this:
Does she like . . .?
Yes, she does./No, she doesn't.

Now ask and answer for Paul in the same way.

4.	Diana likes children and she likes babies, too. Paul likes children, but he doesn't like babies very much. Paul doesn't like cats or dogs very much.

Talk and write about Diana, Paul and your partner's likes and dislikes in the same way.

Are these true or false?
They have coffee in the
    hotel.
Joanne likes Los Angeles.
Paul likes London.

🔊 Dialogue: Part 2

JOANNE: Where do you live?
PAUL: In Manchester.
JOANNE: Is that in the north of England?
PAUL: Yes, it's in the north-west. You live on the west coast, don't you?
JOANNE: Yes. I live in the centre of Los Angeles.

Are these true or false?
Manchester is in the north-west of England.
Los Angeles is on the west coast of America.

North

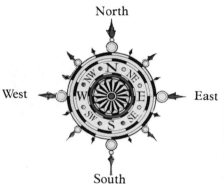

West ← → East

South

Set 3   Places: location (1)

1.   Where do you live?
In Manchester.
Where's that?
It's in the north-west of England.

Ask and answer in pairs. Say where you live.

2.   Diana lives in Manchester, in the north-west of England.
Joanne lives in Los Angeles, on the west coast of America.

Tell the class where your partner lives.

3.   Where does Paul live?
He lives in the north-west of England.
Where do Lucy and Andrew live?
They live in the south of England.

Look at the map of Britain and say where these people live. Ask and answer in pairs.

Robin – Newcastle
Lucy and Andrew – Brighton
Kate – Norwich

Kevin – Exeter
Sarah and Clive – Dover
John and Mary – Liverpool

📼 Dialogue: Part 3

JOANNE: What do you do?
PAUL: I'm a cameraman, but I'm also Diana's assistant.
JOANNE: Oh, what does she do?
PAUL: She's a director. We work for a company called Focus Film and Video. We make documentary films.

Are these true or false?
Diana is an assistant.
Paul is a cameraman.
Focus Film and Video make documentary films.

Set 4   Jobs

1.	
What do you do?	What does she do?
I'm a cameraman.	She's a director.
I work for a company called	What does he do?
I'm a student.	He's Diana's assistant.
I study in London.	I don't know.

Ask and answer about each other in the same way.

2. Find the people in the picture.

Tom is a waiter.
Rashid is a doctor.
James is a secretary.
Eva is a computer programmer.
Ramon is a teacher.

Marisa is a student.
Doris is a housewife.
Sally is an artist.
Tina is an engineer.

Ask and answer about the people, like this:
Is Ramon a student?
No, he isn't.
What does he do?
He's a teacher.
Oh, really?

1. Ramon/student?
2. Rashid/waiter?
3. Sally/housewife?
4. Marisa/engineer?
5. Doris/teacher?
6. James/computer programmer?
7. Eva/doctor?
8. Tom/artist?
9. Tina/secretary?

3. Look at the questions in Exercise 2 again. Write the answers, like this:

1. Ramon isn't a student.   He's a teacher.
2. Rashid isn't . . . .   He's a . . . .
3. Sally isn't . . . .   She's a . . . .

4. Write about three people you know, like this:

My friend, Helen, is a . . . .
My brother, ...
My sister, ...

JOANNE: Vince and I both work for a video company called S and S.

PAUL: S and S? I don't understand. What does that mean?

JOANNE: It means Sight and Sound. Ah, here's a nice place. Let's have a cup of coffee here.

Set 5 The alphabet

Aa Bb Cc Dd Ee Ff Gg Hh Ii Jj Kk Ll Mm Nn Oo
Pp Qq Rr Ss Tt Uu Vv Ww Xx Yy Zz

1. Practise the sounds of the letters:

/eɪ/	/iː/	/e/	/aɪ/	/əʊ/	/uː/	/ɑː/
A	B	F	I	O	Q	R
H	C	L	Y		U	
J	D	M			W	
K	E	N				
	G	S				
	P	X				
	T	Z				
	V					

2. Read these airline names. Say which country or countries they are from.

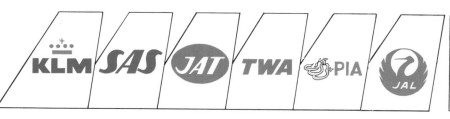

Scandinavia
Japan
Pakistan
Holland
Yugoslavia
America

Read these registration plates:

MMP 270X   DWV 290W   BAS 313X

LRO 844X

JAS 166Y

3. Ask your partner how to spell his or her surname and address. Ask and answer, like this:

What's your surname?
It's BAKER.
How do you spell that?
B-A-K-E-R.

What's your address?
It's 43, Tavistock Road.
How do you spell Tavistock?
T-A-V-I-S-T-O-C-K.

🔲 Open dialogue

Talk to Paul.

PAUL: Hello! I'm Paul. Paul Roberts. What's your name?
YOU: . . . .
PAUL: How do you spell your surname?
YOU: . . . .
PAUL: What do you do?
YOU: . . . .
PAUL: Are you English?
YOU: . . . .
PAUL: Well, I'm English. I'm from Manchester. That's in the north-west of England. Where are you from?
YOU: . . . .
PAUL: And do you like your English classes?
YOU: . . . .
PAUL: Good! Well, goodbye for now!
YOU: . . . .

Roleplay

In pairs. You meet at a party. Ask questions to find out about each other. One of you is Sandra and one of you is Jeremy.

Name:	Sandra Macey	Jeremy Hutchins
Nationality:	American	British
Home town:	Boston, on the east coast of America	Brighton, on the south coast of England
Job:	student nurse	engineer
Likes:	pop and classical music	classical music but not pop music
	Chinese food	Italian food

🔲 Listening

Angela is looking for a job. A man at a job agency takes down some information about her. Complete the information on this form.

SURNAME (Block Capitals)..MR/MRS/MISS
FIRST NAMES...
ADDRESS ....
....
....
PRESENT OR PREVIOUS OCCUPATION ....
TELEPHONE NUMBER ....

Reading

My name is Georgina, but I'm called 'Georgie' by my friends. I live near York, in the north-east of England. I'm a dental nurse. I work for a young Australian dentist. He's very nice and he's a very good dentist, but I don't like my job very much.

My sister is called Rosie. She's married with two children, a girl and a boy, and lives in a house near London, in a town called Enfield. She's a teacher. She teaches in a big school in the north of London. She likes her job very much.

My brother's name is Andrew. He doesn't have a job. He's unemployed.

Answer:

About Georgina:
What is Georgina called by her friends?
Where does she live?
Does she live with her sister?
What does she do?
Does she like her job?

About the dentist:
Is the dentist a man or a woman?
Does Georgina like him?

About her sister:
What is her sister's name?
Is she married?
What does she do?
Where does she work?
Does she like her job?
Does she live in London?
Does she live in a flat or a house?

About her brother:
What does Georgina's brother do?
What's his name?

Writing

Write a few sentences about you and a friend, or your brother or sister.

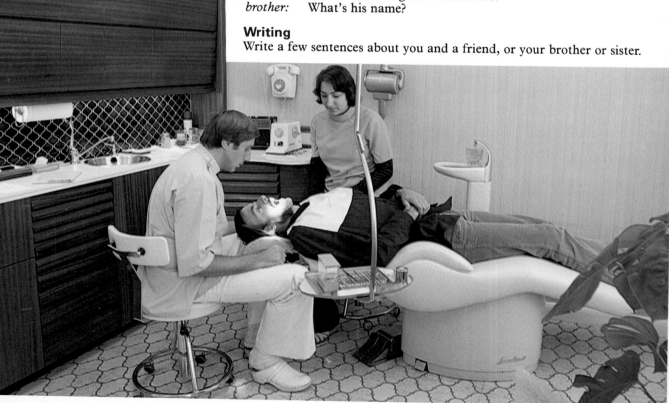

Oral exercises

1. Say what you like (Open exercise)
Do you like pop music?
Yes, I do./No, I don't.

1. pop music?	4. your job?
2. classical music?	5. English classes?
3. cats?	6. your home town?

2. Ask about likes and dislikes
Ask if Diana likes classical music.
Does Diana like classical music?
Yes, she does.
Ask if Paul likes pop music.
Does Paul like pop music?
Yes, he does.

1. Diana/classical music?	4. Diana/babies?
2. Paul/pop music?	5. Diana/dogs?
3. Paul/children?	6. Paul/cats?

3. Answer about likes and dislikes
Say what Diana likes or doesn't like.
Does she like children?
Yes, she does.

1. children?/yes	4. cats?/yes
2. pop music?/no	5. babies?/yes
3. classical music?/yes	6. dogs?/no

4. Ask for personal information
What's Diana's surname?
It's Trent.
What's Diana's telephone number?
I don't know.

1. Diana/surname
2. Diana/telephone number
3. Paul/surname
4. Joanne/address
5. Mr Hall/first name
6. Joanne/telephone number

5. Say where places are
Where's Bristol?
It's in the south-west of England.

1. Bristol/SW	4. Dover/SE
2. Manchester/NW	5. Brighton/S
3. Norwich/E	6. Newcastle/N

Grammar

Do	you they	like	pop music? cats? babies?
Does	he she		

Yes,	I	do.
No,	we they	don't.
Yes,	he	does.
No,	she	doesn't

I We They	like don't like	pop music cats babies children	very much.
He She	likes doesn't like		

Where	do	you they	live? work?
	does	he she	
What	do you		do?
	does	he she	

I We They	live work	in	London. the centre of town.
He She	lives works		
I'm He's	a	teacher. cameraman.	
She's	an	engineer. artist.	

Diana's surname is Trent.
My brother's name is Andrew.

🔊 Dialogue: Part 1

PAUL: Do you want coffee or tea?
JOANNE: Coffee, please. A black coffee.
PAUL: Cake? Biscuits?
JOANNE: No, thanks. Just a coffee.
PAUL: Well, I want a piece of chocolate cake.
Can I have two coffees, please — one black and one white — and a piece of chocolate cake.
BOY: There you are.
PAUL: Thanks. How much is that?
BOY: That's 95 pence, please. Thank you.

Are these true or false?

Paul has a cup of black coffee and a piece of cake.
Joanne has a cup of black coffee.
Joanne has a cup of black coffee and a piece of chocolate cake.
Paul has a cup of white coffee and a piece of chocolate cake.

10 ten
11 eleven
12 twelve
13 thirteen
14 fourteen
15 fifteen
16 sixteen
17 seventeen
18 eighteen
19 nineteen
20 twenty
21 twenty-one
22 twenty-two
30 thirty
40 forty
50 fifty
60 sixty
70 seventy
80 eighty
90 ninety
100 a hundred
1,000 a thousand

$\frac{1}{4}$ = a quarter $\frac{1}{2}$ = a half
$1\frac{1}{2}$ = one and a half
1,000,000 a million

Menu

	Price
Sandwiches	
Cheese	30
Cheese and tomato	35
Egg	30
Beef	40
Cakes and biscuits	
Biscuits (packet)	15
Chocolate cake (piece)	45
Beverages	
Tea	20
Coffee	25
Milk	15
Orange juice	20
Coca-cola, Pepsi-cola, Fanta, 7-up, Mineral water	25

Set 1 Food, drink and money

1.	Do you want coffee or tea? Coffee, please.

5p = five p or five pence
20p = twenty p or twenty pence
£1 = a pound
£1.50 = one pound fifty (pence)
£5 = five pounds

Look at the menu. Offer two things each time. Ask and answer in pairs, like this:

Do you want a cheese sandwich or an egg sandwich?
An egg sandwich, please.

2.	I want a cheese sandwich and a cup of tea. a glass of milk.

Say what you want to eat and drink from the menu in the same way.

3.	How much is that? That's 95 pence, please.

Ask and answer about these prices:

Finger-touch calculator
1/100 chrono/Dual time
CASIO
International £1·99, WALTON'S 34P
NORMAL PRICE £11·75
REDUCED PRICE
Chic £29·95 £6·50
£150—00

4.	How much is a cup of coffee? It's 25 pence. How much is a cheese sandwich? It's 30 pence.

Look at the menu and ask and answer about the following:

1. a cup of tea
2. a piece of cake
3. an egg sandwich
4. a Coca-cola
5. a glass of orange juice
6. a beef sandwich

5.	How much is this/that map? It's . . . . How much are these/those diaries. They're . . . .

Ask and answer about the following in the same way:

THIS/THESE
map (£1.50)
pens (75p)
pencils (25p)
exercise books (35p)

THAT/THOSE
dictionary (£2.99)
box of chocolates (£3.80)
combs (45p)
diaries (£1.90)

6.	Can I have two coffees, please? Yes, that's 50 pence, please.

Ask for the following:

1. a map and a pencil
2. a tea and a glass of orange juice
3. a glass of milk and a packet of biscuits
4. three combs and two pens
5. a tea, a coffee, a piece of cake and a packet of biscuits

29

🔊 Dialogue: Part 2

PAUL: Sugar?
JOANNE: No, thanks.
PAUL: What do you like doing in your spare time, Joanne?
JOANNE: Oh, I like doing lots of things. I like going to the movies. I love skiing. Can you ski?
PAUL: No, I can't.
JOANNE: Really? It's great fun.
PAUL: Do you like sightseeing?
JOANNE: Yes, I do.
PAUL: So do I. But Diana hates it.

Activity	You	Your partner
Reading		
Writing letters		
Sitting in cafés		
Walking round the town		
Going to the cinema		
Going to the theatre		
Going to parties		
Going to discos		
Going to see friends		
Watching television at home		

Set 2 Likes and dislikes (2)

What do you like doing in your spare time?
Look at the chart on the left.

1.	Do you like reading?	Yes, I do. (Very much) Yes, I love it.
	Do you like writing letters?	No, I don't. (Not very much) No, I hate it.

Ask your partner what (s)he likes doing and note down the answer.

2.	I like reading. Yes, so do I./Really? I don't.
	I don't like writing letters. No, nor do I./Really? I do.

Go round the class. See how many people like the same things.

3. Write some sentences and say what you and your partner like and don't like, like this:

> I like going to the cinema and going to the theatre, but I don't like going to discos very much.
> Maria loves going to discos, but she doesn't like watching television very much.

4.	I like John McEnroe. Yes, I like him, too. Really? I don't like him at all.	I like the Muppets. Yes, I like them, too. Really? I don't like them at all.
	I like Olivia Newton-John. Yes, I like her, too. Really? I don't like her at all.	I like Brooke Shields. Who's Brooke Shields? She's an American film star.

In pairs, talk about people you know in the same way.

Set 3   Skills and sports

1. **Can you ski?**

Yes, I can. Can you?
Yes, but not very well. Can you?
No, I can't. Can you?

Look at these sports.

ski

windsurf

roller skate

swim

play tennis

Find out what your friends in your class can do, like this:

Can you ski/play tennis/swim/windsurf/rollerskate?
Yes, I can./No, I can't. Can you?

Note down their answers and then write like this:

In my class, twelve people can ski, two people can rollerskate,
eight people can play tennis, all the class can swim.
No one can windsurf.

2. **Answer these questions about yourself:**
   Can you drive?
   Can you ride a horse?
   Can you speak French?
   Can you cook?
   Can you type?
   Can you play chess?
   Can you play the piano?

Now ask your partner the same questions.

🔊 Dialogue: Part 3

JOANNE: London is an interesting city. I love these streets. How old is St Paul's Cathedral?

PAUL: It's about three hundred years old, I think. Well, here's the hotel.

DIANA: Paul! You're late! We have a meeting.

PAUL: Sorry, Diana.

DIANA: That's all right.

PAUL: See you later, Joanne.

JOANNE: Yes, so long! And thanks for the coffee.

PAUL: (to Diana) Mmm. I like her. She's nice. She's very nice!

Are these true or false?
St Paul's Cathedral isn't very old.
Paul is late for his meeting.
Paul likes Joanne.

Set 4   Age

How old is it?
It's about 300 years old.

How old is he?
He's ten (years old).

How old is she?
She's twenty-four.

Look at the pictures below. Ask and answer questions, like this:

How old is he/she/it?
He/she/it's . . .
How old are they?

He's . . . and she's . . . .
They're . . . .

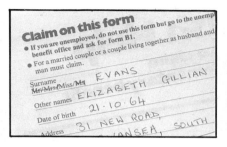

 Open dialogue

Talk to Paul in a coffee bar.

PAUL: Hello.
YOU: . . . .
PAUL: Let's have a drink. Do you want coffee or coke?
YOU: . . . .
PAUL: Do you want a biscuit or a piece of cake with it?
YOU: . . . .
PAUL: OK. Listen! That's a new record by Haircut 100. Do you like it?
YOU: . . . .
PAUL: What sort of music do you like?
YOU: . . . .
PAUL: So do I. What do you like doing in your spare time?
YOU: . . . .
PAUL: Really? I like going to see friends and driving my car. Can you drive?
YOU: . . . .
PAUL: Let's play a record. What do you want?
YOU: . . . .
PAUL: Great! I love that record, too.

Roleplay

In groups of five or six. One of you is working in a coffee bar. The others are customers. Choose from the menu on page 28. You may order separately or together. Order something to drink and something to eat.

📼 Listening

A Swedish girl applies for a job as a home-help with a family in London.
Listen and answer the questions with a tick in the right column, Yes or No

Name: Karin Hallberg	Yes	No
Does she like children?		
Can she cook?		
Does she speak English?		
Can she drive?		
Does she smoke?		
Does she like pop music?		
classical music?		
reading?		
Other interests?		
Does she get the job?		

Reading

WANTED PENFRIENDS
French boy 15, wants penfriends from all over the world. Please write in English. Likes sports, films, pop music. Write to
Jean Ploton Box 234

10 Trafalgar Road,
Solihull,
Birmingham.
10th March, 198

Dear Jean,
Hello! I'm seventeen years old. I'm German and I'm a student. I study in Birmingham.
I like reading, writing letters and going to the cinema, but I don't like cooking. I speak English, German and a little French. I like sports very much, too. I love windsurfing in the summer. Can you windsurf? It's great fun!
Write soon.
Gisela (Hanz)
p.s. I don't smoke. Do you?

Fill in the details about Gisela:

Full name:	
Address:	
Age:	
Nationality:	
Likes:	
Dislikes:	
Sports:	
Languages:	

Writing

Write a similar letter to Jean and tell him about yourself.

Oral exercises

1. Ask what people like
Ask if Paul likes sightseeing.
Does Paul like sightseeing?
Yes, he does.

1. Paul/sightseeing?	4. Vince/windsurfing?
2. Diana/skiing?	5. Paul/writing letters?
3. Joanne/cooking?	6. Diana/playing tennis?

2. Agree with people
I like cooking.
Yes, so do I.
I don't like writing letters.
No, nor do I.

1. I like cooking.
2. I don't like writing letters.
3. I hate sightseeing.
4. I don't like watching television.
5. I love windsurfing.
6. I don't like shopping.

3. Disagree with people
I love going to the theatre.
Really? I don't.
I don't like going to discos very much.
Really? I do.

1. I love going to the theatre.
2. I don't like going to discos very much.
3. I don't like shopping.
4. I love going to concerts.
5. I like watching TV, too.
6. I don't like going to parties at all!

4. Talk about activities and skills (Open exercise)
Do you like sightseeing?
(Yes, I do./No, I don't.)
Can you ski?
(Yes, I can./No, I can't.)

1. Do you like sightseeing?
2. Can you ski?
3. Can you windsurf?
4. Do you like going to discos?
5. Do you like writing letters?
6. Can you drive?

5. Order food and drink
Tea for me, please.
OK. Can I have two teas, please?

1. tea	4. a cheese sandwich
2. coffee	5. a piece of chocolate cake
3. coke	6. a glass of mineral water

6. Ask the price
Ask how much the egg sandwich is.
How much is that egg sandwich?
It's 30 pence.
Ask how much the biscuits are.
How much are those biscuits?
They're 15 pence a packet.

1. egg sandwich	4. chocolate cake
2. biscuits	5. cheese sandwich
3. cheese and tomato sandwiches	6. chocolate biscuits

Grammar

Can	you he she	ski? drive? speak French?	Yes, No,	I he she	can. can't.
I He She	can't	ski drive speak French	very well.		

Can	I we	have	two coffees a Coca-cola	please?

How much	is	this map? that dictionary?
	are	these sandwiches? those biscuits?

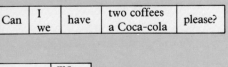

I like	me. it. him. her.
He likes	them. you.

I want a	cup glass piece	of	coffee. water. cake.

I	(don't) like hate love	going to school. writing letters. cooking.
He She	hates loves	

How old	is	are you? he? she? it?	I'm He's She's It's	22 (years old). a hundred years old.

35

Name: Dean Hudson
Age: 39
Nationality: American
Job: sports writer
Married: yes, to Lynne, a history teacher
Children: three boys, aged 5, 8, 11
Home: a house in Denver, Colorado
Likes: cooking, classical music
Dislikes: winter, washing up, smoking
Favourite
holiday place: London, or
                 Central America

Name: Magdalena Planchos
Age: 35
Nationality: Mexican
Job: assistant director of a language
                 school
Married: yes, to Carlos, an engineer
Children: two boys, aged 10 and 13
Likes: teaching English, America,
                 watching old American films
Dislikes: beer and cooking
Favourite
holiday place: the United States

THE ··PEOPLE·· GAME

Name: Della Freeman
Age: 17
Nationality: British
Job: student at a college of
                 engineering
Married: no
Home: lives with her married sister in
                 South London
Likes: meeting people from other
                 countries, writing letters
Dislikes: watching TV
Favourite
holiday place: Italy

Name: Angelo Milazzo
Age: 18
Nationality: Italian
Job: university student of economics
Married: no
Likes: meeting new people, Diana Ross
Dislikes: American TV films
Favourite
holiday place: Sardinia
Home: in a student hostel

Name: Terri Lichère
Age: 19
Nationality: Canadian
Job: Embassy secretary in Quebec
                 in Canada
Married: no
Home: in a flat in Quebec with two
                 other secretaries
Likes: cooking, swimming, skiing
Dislikes: watching football on
                 television
Favourite
holiday place: the Greek islands

Name: Paloma Jerez
Age: 27
Nationality: Spanish
Job: teacher of mathematics
Married: yes, to Juan, a dentist
Children: two girls, aged 3 (twins)
Home: in a flat in Madrid
Likes: going to parties, swimming,
                 playing the classical guitar
Dislikes: watching TV
Favourite
holiday place: Ibiza

Roleplay

Divide, as near as you can, into groups of eight (but no more than eight). Read about the people. Decide which person you want to be. You must each choose a different person. Study the details of your new character.

Find a new friend in your group: someone who likes the same things you like and does the same things you do. This is what you do:
1. Greet people and introduce yourself.
2. Ask where people come from and what nationality they are.
3. Ask what languages they speak.
4. Ask what they do.
5. Ask about their likes and dislikes.
6. Ask about their favourite holiday places.

Writing

Make a chart for someone in your class and fill in the details.

Name: Pierre Dumas
Age: 26
Nationality: French
Job: works in a supermarket
Married: yes, to Suzanne, a hairdresser
Children: a girl, aged 3
Home: in a flat in the centre of Nantes,
                 in north-west France
Likes: American rock music, American food
Dislikes: spaghetti, beer
Favourite
holiday place: Corsica (Club
                 Mediterranée)

Name: Irma Ulriksson
Age: 30
Nationality: Swedish
Job: director at Swedish Radio
Married: yes, to Bengt, a teacher
Children: Lina 2 and Marcus 4
Home: in a flat in the centre of
                 Stockholm; summer house in
                 the Archipelago
Likes: classical music, playing
                 with the children
Dislikes: war films
Favourite
holiday place: Spain and Portugal

🔊 Listening

1. Look at the people in The People Game on pages 36 and 37. Who is speaking?

2. Listen to these people talking. Write the missing information about them in the chart below.

	HEATHER	GILES
Age:		
Home:		
Special interests:		

3. Listen to this travel agent talking to two Americans about a visit to Stratford-upon-Avon. Number the pieces of information in the order the travel agent mentions them.

The name of the play
The name of the hotel
The travel agent's telephone number
The name of the restaurant
The price of the theatre tickets

4. Listen to this conversation. Answer the questions:

Are Mr Brooks and Miss Barrett
in a hotel?
at an airport?

Are they booking rooms?
a table?

Do they like the food in the restaurant?   Yes/No

Do they like the wine?   Yes/No

How much is the meal altogether?   £14/£40/£4

Reading

1. Mr and Mrs Clark live in Newcastle, in the north-east of England.

5. The Clarks are in a small hotel, but the people in the hotel don't like children.

9. The children don't like the food, nor do Mr and Mrs Clark.

A summer holiday in St Ives

2. They have three children, two boys and a baby girl.

3. It is summer and they want a holiday.
'What about St Ives?'
'Yes, lovely!'

4. St Ives is a very beautiful town by the sea in Cornwall. People like going to St Ives for their holidays.

6. The children play in the restaurant.

7. They talk in the TV room.

8. The baby cries at night.

10. They go swimming, but the water is cold. The children don't like it.

11. It rains every day.
'We want to go home!' the children cry.

12. Every summer many people think:
'Travel east or travel west,
But going home is always best!'

1. Are these true or false?
The Clarks live in the south-west of England.
They go to Newcastle for their summer holidays.
St Ives is a town in Cornwall.
The Clarks stay in a large hotel.
The other people in the hotel don't like the children.

2. Complete these sentences:
The people in the hotel don't like the children because they. . . . .;
they. . . . .; and the baby. . . . .

The Clark family don't like their holiday in Cornwall because they
. . . . food; the water. . . . .; and it . . . . every day.

Reading for information

1. What's the name of the Public
Relations Manager at the Tower Hotel?
Is the Editor in Chief of *Woman*
magazine a man or a woman?
What does George Cannon do?
What does Betty Hale do?

Jill Faulds
Public Relations Manager

St. Katharine's Way,
London E1 9LD
Telephone: 01-481 2575
Cables: Towerhotel London E1
Telex 885934

woman
WHO WE ARE

EDITOR IN CHIEF	Jane Reed
ASSISTANT EDITORS	Billie Figg
	George Cannon
ART EDITOR	Nick Overhead
MANAGING EDITOR	Betty Hale
SENIOR EDITOR	Gaythorne Silvester
FEATURES EDITOR	Dee Nolan
FASHION	Geraldine Gobby
BEAUTY	Arline Usden
HOME	Jane Graining
KNITTING	Lesley Stanfield
COOKERY	Frances Naldrett
FICTION	Rose Wild
TRAVEL & MOTORING	Jean Barratt
YOU & US	Kate Mahony
PICTURES	Barbara Peevor
CHIEF SUB-EDITOR	Linda Belcher
READERS' SERVICE	Terry Austin

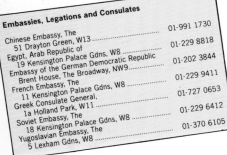

Embassies, Legations and Consulates	
Chinese Embassy, The 51 Drayton Green, W13	01-991 1730
Egypt, Arab Republic of 19 Kensington Palace Gdns, W8	01-229 8818
Embassy of the German Democratic Republic Brent House, The Broadway, NW9	01-202 3844
French Embassy, The 11 Kensington Palace Gdns, W8	01-229 9411
Greek Consulate General, 1a Holland Park, W11	01-727 0653
Soviet Embassy, The 18 Kensington Palace Gdns, W8	01-229 6412
Yugoslavian Embassy, The 5 Lexham Gdns, W8	01-370 6105

2. You are from France. What is the telephone number of your Embassy?
Germany.
China.
Greece.

In which part of London (north, south, east, west) is:
the Soviet Embassy?   the German Embassy?   the Chinese Embassy?

MAKING FRIENDS IN LONDON

parties
discos

pub evenings
wine bars
films
concerts
folk
jazz
ballet
cooking
bridge
chess
football
waterskiing
horseriding

astrology

is a challenge even for the most sociable of us. You can't just go up to strangers and say: 'Hi, I'd like to meet you.'
If you enjoy meeting people LONDON LINKUP could be just what you've been looking for. We are a friendly cross-section of mostly unattached young people aged 20-40, equally divided between the sexes. Our aim is to become involved in things that really interest us and to make worthwhile use of our spare time. There's always lots happening all over London amongst our 1,500 members who organise over 150 events each month.
To find out all about us, just drop into one of our informal introductory talks. These take place at both 6.30pm and 8.00pm on the following days (excluding public holidays)-
Monday and Thursdays. At the International Sportswriters' Club, Great Russell Street. (Opposite the YMCA near Tottenham Court Road tube).
If you would like a chat beforehand, please ring us 01-606 1750. We look forward to welcoming you.

LONDON LINKUP

3. What is there to do in London if you like:
music?   outdoor sports?
meeting people?   indoor games?
the arts?

Which of the list of activities do you like?
Which don't you like?
Which can't you do?

Royal Shakespeare Restaurants

Waterside Stratford-upon-Avon. CV37 6BB England.
Telephone: 0789 293226   VAT Registered No. 313 4205 10

0789 292271
Royal Shakespeare Theatre
A Midsummer Night's Dream

Cast includes:
Jane Carr
Philip Franks
Mike Gwilym
Geoffrey Hutchings
Joseph Marcell
John Rogan
Juliet Stevenson
Simon Templeman
Harriet Walter

Hermia
Lysander
Theseus/Oberon
Bottom
Puck
Quince
Hippolyta/Titania
Demetrius
Helena

Directed by Ron Daniels
Designed by Maria Bjornson
Lighting by Chris Ellis
Music by Stephen Oliver
Choreography by David Toguri

A Midsummer Night's Dream:
Joseph Marcell *Puck* Mike Gwilym *Oberon*

Come to Stratford the easy way—
with The Shakespeare Connection!
A fast rail/road link between
London and Stratford designed to
make your theatre visit an easy one.
Phone Guide Friday on Stratford
(0789) 294466 for further
information.

Royal Shakespeare
Theatre : Stratford

MAY 14
FRIDAY EVE. 7-30
STALLS RIGHT
£8·50 Incl. VAT

4
5
Q 4
351   [P.T.O.

VAT No. 27270/5851
TO BE RETAINED   [P.T.O.

DATE

A Midsummer Night's Dream was most likely
written in late 1594/winter of 1595. It has been
thought that the play was first performed to
celebrate the wedding in a noble family, possibly
that of the Earl of Derby to Elizabeth Vere in
1595.

THE ARDEN HOTEL

Waterside, Stratford-upon-Avon
Tel: 0789 294949

IMMEDIATELY OPPOSITE THE THEATRE AND
OVERLOOKING THE RIVER AVON

Directors: **Mr and Mrs J. N. Anker**
Comfort Hotel International Associate

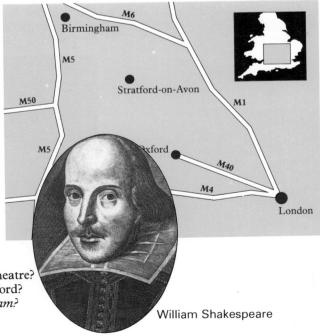

William Shakespeare

4. What is the telephone number of the Arden Hotel?
of the Royal Shakespeare Theatre?
of the tourist office in Stratford?
How many are in the cast of *A Midsummer Night's Dream*?
What are the seat numbers of the tickets?
How much are they?

INTERNATIONAL BUFFET				
Beverages			**Sandwiches**	
Coffee	black	30	Egg	50
	cream	32	Salami	48
Tea		20	Beef	57
Hot chocolate		31	Cheese	52
Milk		19	**Cakes & Pastries**	
Coca Cola		30	Jam doughnut	26
Fanta Orange		30	Danish pastry	34
	Lemon		Coffee cake	42
Orange juice		52	Fresh cream gateau	55
Apple juice		··	Biscuits	20
Orange squash		19		
All prices include VAT				

5. You are in a group of six. Two want black coffees, two want coffee with cream, one wants tea and you want Coca-cola. Three want cheese sandwiches, two want jam doughnuts, and you want a fresh cream gateau with your Coca-cola. How much is it altogether?

Reading and writing
Look at page 37. Read this paragraph about Paloma Jerez.

Paloma Jerez is Spanish. She is married to Juan, a dentist, and lives in a flat in Madrid. She has twins, two girls aged three, and she is a teacher of mathematics. In her spare time she likes going to parties, playing the classical guitar and swimming, but she doesn't like watching television at all. She likes going to Ibiza for her holidays.

Write about Dean and Della in the same way.
Then use the chart about your friend to write a similar paragraph.

Language focus

1. Sort these words into five groups of related words. There are four words in each group.

man	coffee	cinema	doctor	milk
secretary	south	student	east	girl
teacher	boy	west	theatre	tea
woman	north	disco	water	concert

2. Complete the words:

1. Good a_____n.
2. P_____ to m_____ you.
3. W_____ do you live?
4. My a_____ is 23 Tiverton Road, Southall.
5. My t_____n_____ is 574 3355.
6. Do you live in the c_____ of town?
7. I live on the w_____ c_____ of America.
8. I don't have a j_____. I'm u_____.
9. Can I have two c_____, p_____?
10. Do you want an egg s_____,
    or a ch_____ s_____?

**3. Put the words in the right order.
Start each sentence with a capital letter.**

1. you meet pleased to.
2. much Americans like I very.
3. two please have I can coffees?
4. time do your spare like you what doing in?
5. Scotland of he the lives north in.
6. coffee you tea or do want?
7. Roberts name your is David?
8. much these how cheese are sandwiches?
9. the summer I windsurfing in love.
10. three with married she is children.

4. Complete the conversation:

SANDRA: Hello, Jim.
JIM: Oh, ... How. . . . . .?
SANDRA: . . . . . . thanks, and . . . . . .?
JIM: Oh, I'm . . . . . . How's Martin?
SANDRA: He's OK. He's at home with the children.
JIM: . . . . . . the children now?
SANDRA: Damian's seven and Lucy's four.
JIM: Really! And what do . . . . . . now? Are you
     still a teacher?
SANDRA: Yes, ... And . . . . . . you still like your job
        at Shell?
JIM: No, I . . . . . . very much.
SANDRA: Oh. I'm sorry. You must talk to Martin. He
        . . . . . . like his job much, either. Well, I must
        go now.
JIM: Yes, I must, too. Look after yourself, and
     come and see us sometime.

5. Which is correct, a, b or c?

1. What's the man's
   name?
   a) It's name's Pat.
   b) His name's Pat.
   c) Her name's Pat.

2. What's she called?
   a) She's Sally.
   b) Sally.
   c) It's Sally.

3. Are you English?
   a) Yes, he is.
   b) Yes, they are.
   c) Yes, I am.

4. What nationality are
   they?
   a) The Americans.
   b) He's American.
   c) They're American.

5. What does she do?
   a) She's an artist.
   b) She's in London.
   c) She's English.

6. a) What does he do?   He's an engineer.
   b) How do you do?
   c) What is he doing?

7. Do you like Vince?
   a) Yes, he does.
   b) Yes, I like her very much.
   c) Yes, I do. I like him very
      much.

8. What do you do in
   your spare time?
   a) Yes, I do.
   b) I like swimming.
   c) I like doing it.

9. a) How much are those   They're 70 pence a kilo.
      oranges?
   b) How is this
      orange?
   c) How much is it?

10. How old is she?
    a) She has four.
    b) It's her birthday.
    c) She is four years old.

🔊 **Dialogue: Part 1**

VINCE: Hi, you guys!
DIANA: Hello, Vince.
VINCE: Were you two at the conference this morning?
DIANA: No, we weren't. I was at a meeting and Paul was in town — with Joanne.
VINCE: Oh.

DIANA: How was the conference?
VINCE: It was interesting.
DIANA: Oh! Look at the time! I must go. I want to go to the bank.
PAUL: And I want to buy some toothpaste. See you later, Vince!

Answer yes or no.
Was Vince at the conference in the morning?
Was Joanne with Vince?
Were Diana and Paul there?
Were Paul and Joanne together?

Set 1 Past time

1.	Were	you	at the conference	this morning?	Yes,	I was.	
		they		yesterday?	Yes,	we they	were.
					No,	I wasn't. they weren't.	
	Was	he she	in London	last week? last night?	Yes, he was. No, she wasn't.		

Diana
at a
meeting

Vince
at the
conference

Joanne and
Paul in town

The Japanese
tourists at the
Japanese Embassy

Was Joanne at the conference this morning? No, she wasn't.
Was she in town with Paul? Yes she was.

Ask and answer two questions about Diana, Vince, Paul and Joanne and the Japanese tourists, in the same way.

2.	Where were you yesterday?
	I was at a meeting.

Ask and answer questions about the people, like this:

Where was Vince this morning?
He was at the conference.

Where were Paul and Joanne this morning?
They were in town.

3.	How was the conference yesterday?
	It was interesting.
	How was the party last night?
	It was fun.

Ask and answer questions about the following:

the lecture   the disco   the film   the TV programme

4. Ask your partner:

Were you here yesterday?
Were you here last week?
Were you early for class/work this morning?
Where were you last night?
What was on TV last night? Was it interesting?

Set 2 Shops and requirements

1.	I want to	buy	a film.	
		get	some	toothpaste.
				shoes.

Match these things with their illustrations.

stamps	toothpaste	film	chocolates
shoes	cassette	book about Britain	map
money	postcard	newspaper	soap

Tell your partner three things you want to buy or get.

2. Look at the pictures below. Match each shop or building with its right name.

a bank	a shoe shop	a chemist's	a newsagent's
a book shop	a record shop	a post office	

Say where you want to go for each item in Exercise 1, like this:

(stamps) I want to go to a post office.

3. Look at Paul and Diana's lists and tell your partner where they want to go, like this:

(toothpaste) Paul wants to go to a chemist's.

Toothpaste
Postcards
Stamps

Money
Map
Shoes

🔊 Dialogue: Part 2

DIANA: Let's ask that man.
PAUL: Excuse me. Is there a bank near here?
MAN: Yes. There's one over there, next to the newsagent's. It's opposite the record shop.
DIANA: Thanks.
PAUL: And where can I buy a film for my camera?
MAN: At the chemist's. There's one opposite the post office.

PAUL: I'm sorry, but where's the post office?
MAN: Are you strangers here?
DIANA: We're from Manchester.
MAN: How funny! I was there last week. Well, turn left at the pizza bar and the chemist's is on your right.
DIANA: Thank you very much.
MAN: You're welcome.

Set 3   Places: location (2)

record shop	travel agent's	flower shop
bank	shoe shop	Odeon cinema
video shop	wine bar	book shop
newsagent's	post office	café
chemist's	pizza bar	

	Record Shop	Bank		
	Video Shop	News-agent's		
Chemist's		Travel Agent's	Shoe Shop	Wine Bar
Post Office		Pizza Bar	Flower Shop	Odeon Cinema
Book Shop		Café		

1. Talk about the places on the plan, like this:
There's a record shop.
There's a . . . .

2. Is there a bank near here?
Yes. There's one next to the newsagent's.

Ask for these places in the shopping centre. Answer with next to.

a record shop	a video shop	a cinema
a wine bar	a newsagent's	a café
a book shop	a shoe shop	

3. Is there a chemist's near here?
Yes. There's one opposite the post office.

Ask for these places. Answer with opposite.

a record shop	a flower shop	a travel agent's	a wine bar
a cinema	a book shop	a post office	a pizza bar

4. Where can I buy a film?
At the chemist's.
Turn left at the pizza bar and it's on your right.

You are outside the cinema. Ask where you can buy the following. Answer giving directions.

a newspaper	a book about London
a cassette	a cup of tea and a sandwich

5. Look at the dialogue and the plan again. Work in pairs. One of you is a stranger and one of you lives in the town. You are outside the cinema. You want a record shop and you want to get some stamps. Write out the conversations afterwards.

PAUL: What time is it now?
The bank closes at
half past three.

DIANA: It's twenty past.
Let's hurry. The lecture
starts at four o'clock.

Are these true or false?
It is half past three.
The bank closes at twenty past
three.
The lecture starts at three o'clock.

Set 4   Clock times

| two o'clock | quarter past two (two fifteen) | half past two (two thirty) | quarter to three (two forty-five) | three o'clock |

| five past three | twenty past three | twenty-five past three | twenty-five to four | twenty to four | ten to four | five to four |

1.   What time is it?   It's two o'clock.
What's the time?   It's twenty past three.

Look at the times below. Ask and answer in pairs in the same way:

2.   Is it five o'clock?   No, it's ten past.
Is it seven o'clock?   No, it's ten to.

Ask and answer about the clocks in Exercise 1 in the same way.

Set 5 Fixed times

Train information

	OPEN	CLOSE
BANK	9.30 a.m.	3.30 p.m.
POST OFFICE	9.00 a.m.	5.00 p.m.
NEWSAGENT	8.30 a.m.	6.00 p.m.
	START	FINISH
FILM	8.25 p.m.	10.45 p.m.
CONCERT	7.30 p.m.	9.45 p.m.
FOOTBALL MATCH	3.00 p.m.	4.45 p.m.
	LEAVE	ARRIVE
BUS	2.10 p.m.	2.20 p.m.
TRAIN	4.15 p.m.	10.25 p.m.
PLANE	12.35 p.m.	4.40 p.m.

Note: a.m. = in the morning
p.m. = in the afternoon or evening

1.	The bank opens at half past nine and closes at half past three.

Talk about the times like this. Then write some sentences.

2.	What time When	does the bank open?	It opens at	half past nine. nine thirty.

Ask and answer about the times in the same way.

3. Write notes like this for the film, the concert and the train.

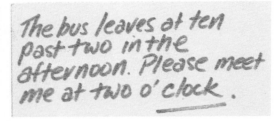

The bus leaves at ten past two in the afternoon. Please meet me at two o'clock.

🔊 Open dialogue
Talk to Vince.

VINCE: Hi, there! How are you?
YOU: . . . .
VINCE: Fine, thanks. What time is it?
YOU: . . . .
VINCE: Is it? I want to send a parcel to the States. Is there a post office near here?
YOU: . . . .
VINCE: And where can I rent a car?
YOU: . . . .
VINCE: OK. What time does your class finish today?
YOU: . . . .
VINCE: What do you want to do after your class?
YOU: . . . .
VINCE: OK. See you soon. Bye!

LONDON HEATHROW AIRPORT DOMESTIC Passenger Timetable	Airline	Flight No.	Day	Dep.	Arr.
Edinburgh	BE	BE916	Daily	0840	0925
Edinburgh	BE	BE4483	Daily	1835	1920
Newcastle	DA	DA052	Daily	0750	0835
Newcastle	DA	DA056	Daily	1800	1845
Birmingham	DA	DA053	Daily	1900	1935

Roleplay

In pairs or groups. You are at a travel agency. The travel agent has a timetable of flights from London to other big cities in Britain. Choose one of the following situations and act out the conversation with the travel agent:

1. You want to go to Edinburgh. You want to be there before 10 a.m.
2. You want to go to Newcastle. You want to be there before 7.30 p.m.
3. You want to go to Birmingham. You want to be there before 8 p.m.

Follow this guide:

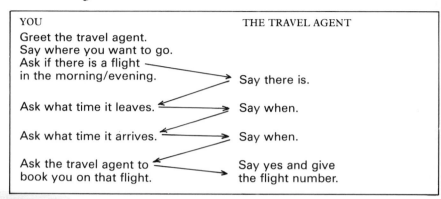

YOU — THE TRAVEL AGENT

Greet the travel agent.
Say where you want to go.
Ask if there is a flight in the morning/evening. → Say there is.
Ask what time it leaves. ↔ Say when.
Ask what time it arrives. ↔ Say when.
Ask the travel agent to book you on that flight. ↔ Say yes and give the flight number.

St. Katharine's Way, London E1 9LD
Telephone: 01-481 2575
Cables: Towerhotel London E1
Telex: 885934

Friday evening

Darling James,

How are you? How's Delia? I hope you are both well. I miss you very much.

The flight to London was fine and the Tower Hotel is very comfortable. The conference is quite interesting, but I am very busy. Yesterday Paul and I were at a meeting with some American people - a man from World Video, and a girl from CBS in New York. The girl was very interesting and I want to meet her again. Also I want to see Douglas Kennedy. He's a director at the BBC and he wants to see our film.

Tell Delia there's a restaurant next to the hotel and it has lovely chocolate ice-cream!

See you soon.

Lots of love,

Diana
xxx

Listening

Paul telephones a friend and asks him to go to the cinema. Listen and note down the answers:

What film does Paul want to see?
What time does the programme start?
What time does the main film start?
What is the name of the cinema?
What street is it in?

Reading

Read the letter and answer:

How was Diana's flight?
Is the Tower Hotel comfortable?
Is the conference good?
When was Paul and Diana's meeting?
Who was the meeting with?
Who is Douglas Kennedy?
What does he want to see?
Where is the restaurant?

Writing

Read this information about banks and shops in Britain.

In Britain, banks open at nine thirty and close at three thirty. They open five days a week. Most shops open at nine o'clock and close at five thirty or six in the evening. Some shops in small towns close early one day a week. In London, many shops are open until seven or eight o'clock one night a week. This is called 'late night shopping.'

Now write a paragraph about the opening and closing times of banks and shops in your country.

Oral exercises

1. Check people's movements
Were you at the conference this morning?
At the conference? No, I wasn't.
Were they at the hotel last night?
At the hotel? No, they weren't.
1. you/at the conference this morning?
2. they/at the hotel last night?
3. they/at the embassy yesterday?
4. you/in town last night?
5. she/with you this morning?
6. they/at the meeting last week?

2. Say where places and shops are
Excuse me, but is there a bank near here?
Bank? Yes. There's one over there.
1. bank   4. flower shop
2. post office   5. book shop
3. restaurant   6. video shop

3. Ask about places and shops
Ask for a bank.
Is there a bank near here?
Yes, next to the newsagent's.
1. bank/newsagent's   4. record shop/video shop
2. shoe shop/wine bar   5. café/flower shop
3. book shop/pizza bar   6. cinema/flower shop

4. Give exact locations
Is the bank opposite the newsagent's?
No. It's next to the newsagent's.

Is the pizza bar next to the travel agent's?
No. It's opposite the travel agent's.
1. bank/opposite/newsagent's?
2. pizza bar/next to/travel agent's?
3. cinema/opposite/flower shop?
4. post office/next to/chemist's?
5. record shop/opposite/video shop?
6. flower shop/next to/pizza bar?

5. Give fixed times
Does the bus leave at five to, or five past, four?
It leaves at five past.
Does the train arrive at ten past, or ten to, three?
It arrives at ten to.
1. bus/leave/five to, or five past, four?
2. train/arrive/ten past, or ten to, three?
3. film/start/twenty past, or half past, seven?
4. match/finish/five o'clock, or quarter to?
5. bank/open/nine o'clock, or half past?
6. shop/close/half past five, or six?

6. Ask about fixed times
Ask when the bus leaves.
Excuse me, but what time does the bus leave?
At half past ten.
1. bus/leave/10.30   4. post office/close/5.30
2. Newcastle train/arrive/5.00 5. match/finish/4.00
3. main film/start/2.30   6. bank/open/9.30

Grammar

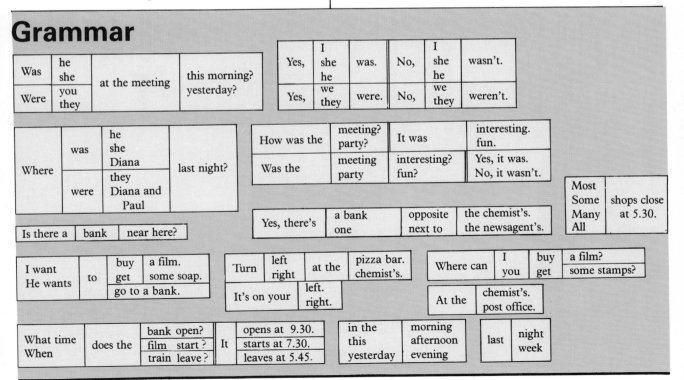

⊙⊙ Dialogue: Part 1

DIANA: Let's walk across the park.
VINCE: Isn't it a lovely day?
DIANA: Yes, it's beautiful.
VINCE: Look at him. What's
       he doing? Is he doing
       a work-out?
DIANA: You mean exercises?
       He's doing yoga, I think.
VINCE: What are those kids doing?

DIANA: They're sailing model boats
       by remote control.
VINCE: Hey, that's neat!

Are these true or false?
Diana and Vince are in the
    street.
It is a nice day.
The man is doing exercises.
Some children are sailing
    model boats.

Set 1 Present activities

1.

What's he doing?	What are they doing?
He's doing yoga.	They're sailing model boats.

Ask and answer about the people in the pictures, like this:

What's she doing?
She's jogging.

waterskiing   cycling   playing tennis   playing football   doing exercises

jogging

2. A teacher is talking about his class and what activities they do:

'Every day we have Free Activity Hour. The children can do what they like. They paint a lot. Some like standing up, some sit at tables and paint, some lie on the floor and paint! They read books, watch television . . . Some like listening to songs or stories on cassette. Others do jigsaws, or play with toys. One or two write stories. All the children love the Free Activity Hour. And so do I. It's great fun!'

Ask and answer about the children in the picture, like this:

What's the boy doing?
He's . . .
What are the girls doing?
They're . . .

3. Look at the picture again. Ask and answer, like this:

Is the boy reading a book?
Yes, he is./No, he isn't. He's . . .

Are the girls sitting?
Yes, they are./No, they aren't. They're . . .

DIANA: Look at her! She's jogging.
VINCE: My wife jogs every morning.
DIANA: Really?
VINCE: Yes, she gets up early. She gets up at six and goes jogging.
DIANA: What? Every day? Even at the weekend?
VINCE: Yes, even on Saturday and Sunday.

Answer:
What is the woman doing?
Does Vince's wife jog?
What time does she get up?
Does she jog every day?

Set 2   Routines

> **1.**   My wife goes jogging every morning.

Match the captions below with the pictures.

After supper she studies.
She has breakfast with the family at half past seven.
Kelly Hall gets up at six o'clock in the morning and goes jogging at half past six.
She makes supper for the children at half past six.
She finishes work at half past four and goes home.
She goes to work at quarter past eight.

Write a paragraph about Kelly Hall's day. Link two sentences each time using and.

1.
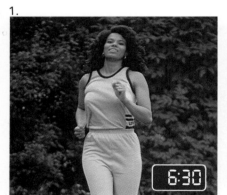

2.

3.

4.

5.

6.

2. In pairs, ask and answer about Kelly's day.
Ask questions like this:

> What time does she get up?
> What does she do before breakfast?
> What time does she have breakfast?
> When does she go to work?

Continue in the same way.

3. Ask and answer about these people's routines:

	gets up at	starts work at	has lunch	finishes work at	after supper	goes to bed at
VINCE	7.00	8.30	in a restaurant	7.00	reads the newspaper, watches TV	11.00
DIANA	7.30	9.30	in the canteen or at home	5.00	puts her child to bed, talks to her husband, James	11.30
JOANNE	7.45	9.00	in a park or at work	6.00	goes to see some friends	11.00 or 12.00
PAUL	8.00	9.30	in a pub or in the canteen	5.00	listens to music, reads, or goes out for a beer	12.00

Write a paragraph describing the daily routine of Vince, Diana, Joanne or Paul, and write one describing your own routine.

4. Days of the week:
Monday Tuesday Wednesday Thursday Friday
Saturday Sunday

Diana and Vince talk about their weekly routines.
Use the information to complete their diaries for a week.

DIANA: On Tuesday evening I go to a French class.
On Friday morning I go swimming before work.
On Saturday we visit my mother.

VINCE: On Monday evening I play squash.
On Wednesday morning I work at home.
On Saturday night my wife and I go out and see friends.
On Sunday morning we go to church and then we go to a restaurant for lunch.

5. What special things do you do on different days of the week?
Ask your partner, too and tell the rest of the class.

		DIANA	VINCE
Monday	a.m.		
	p.m.		
Tuesday	a.m.		
	p.m.		
Wednesday	a.m.		
	p.m.		
Thursday	a.m.		
	p.m.		
Friday	a.m.		
	p.m.		
Saturday	a.m.		
	p.m.		
Sunday	a.m.		
	p.m.		

📼 Dialogue: Part 3

DIANA: Have you got any children?
VINCE: Yes. We've got three kids. Two go to High School and Brad started at UCLA last year. What about you?
DIANA: My daughter is nine. She's called Delia. We've only got one. My husband is looking after her.
VINCE: Look. Paul and Joanne are already there. Can you see them? They're sitting outside the pub.
DIANA: Yes, it's quite hot now, but it was cold this morning.
VINCE: You have really nice weather here.
DIANA: Yes, sometimes!

Answer:
Has Vince got any children?
How old is Diana's daughter?
Where are Paul and Joanne sitting?
What's the weather like?

Set 3 The family

> 1. Have you got any children?
> We've got three children.
> Our son is at college.
> I haven't got any brothers or sisters.

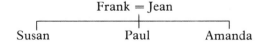

Vince is Kelly's *husband.*
Kelly is Vince's *wife.*
Vince and Kelly are the children's *father and mother.*
They are their *parents.*
Brad and Mick are Carrie's *brothers.*
Carrie is Brad and Mick's *sister.*
Carrie is Vince and Kelly's *daughter.*
Brad and Mick are their *sons.*

Now talk about Paul's family:

```
          Frank = Jean
     ┌─────────┼─────────┐
   Susan      Paul     Amanda
```

2. Work in pairs:
1. One of you is Kelly. Ask her if she has any children.
2. One of you is Brad. Ask him if he has any brothers or sisters.
3. One of you is Frank. Ask if he has any children.
4. One of you is Carrie. Ask if she has any brothers or sisters.
5. One of you is Paul. Ask if he has any brothers or sisters.

3. Ask your partner about his/her family. Ask their names and ages, too. Write a short paragraph about your family.

Set 4 The weather

1.	What's the weather like?	It's	quite very	hot. warm. cold. nice.
				snowing. raining.

In pairs, make remarks about the weather in the pictures, like this:
What's the weather like? It's very hot.

2.		a lovely an awful	day!			
	Isn't it	warm! hot! cold! nice!			Yes, it's	beautiful. terrible.

In pairs, look at the pictures again and make remarks, like this:
Isn't it hot/cold!
Yes, it's beautiful/terrible!

🔊 Open dialogue
Talk to Kelly on the telephone. She's in Los Angeles.

KELLY: Hi! It's really hot here. What's your weather like?
YOU: . . . .
KELLY: It is? And where are you now? What are you doing?
YOU: . . . .
KELLY: Really? What's your routine like now? Do you get up
early every day?
YOU: . . . .
KELLY: Is that so? What time do you go to bed?
YOU: . . . .
KELLY: I like walking along the beach at Santa Monica on
Sundays. What do you like doing?
YOU: . . . .
KELLY: Well, enjoy your lesson! Bye!
YOU: . . . .

🔊 Listening

Listen to these people talking about their daily routines.
Fill in the missing information.

	TERRY a taxi driver	VERONICA a policewoman
get up start work lunch finish work after supper Friday night Sunday		

Reading

The Gomez family live in Mexico City. On Sundays they go to Chapultepec
Park. Look at their photographs and read about their day.

On Sundays we get up early. We don't have a big breakfast, only
coffee and bread and butter. Then we go to church. After church we all go
to Chapultepec Park. This is a big, beautiful park in the centre of the city.

First we go boating on the lake. Then we sit under the trees and have our
picnic lunch. The children fly their kites. I always sleep after lunch
on Sundays!

In the afternoons the small children ride their bicycles. Baby Bianca likes
riding in a little goat cart. You can see one in my photograph.

At about five o'clock we buy fruit or ice cream and then we catch the bus
home.

We have supper at home and then the children go to bed. We usually go
to bed early on Sundays.

Correct these statements:

1. They get up late on Sundays. (No, they don't. They get up early.)
2. They have a big breakfast.
3. They go straight to the park.
4. The park is outside the city.
5. They have lunch on the lake.
6. The children sleep in the afternoon.
7. Baby Bianca likes riding a bicycle.
8. They have fruit and ice cream for supper.
9. They usually go to bed late.

Writing

Write three short paragraphs about your Sunday. Use this guide:

PARAGRAPH 1　When do you get up?
Morning　　　What do you have for breakfast?
　　　　　　　Do you go to church?

PARAGRAPH 2　How do you spend the main part of the day?
Day　　　　　Do you go to a park or a museum, or visit relations?
　　　　　　　Where do you have lunch?
　　　　　　　What do you do after lunch?
　　　　　　　When do you go home?

PARAGRAPH 3　What do you do in the evening?
Evening　　　Where do you have supper?
　　　　　　　What time do you go to bed?

Oral exercises

1. Explain present activities
What are you doing? Are you working?
No, I'm not working now.

1. work
2. read
3. study
4. listen to the radio
5. watch television
6. play with the children

2. Talk about people's exercise routines
Is Michael jogging?
No, he isn't. He doesn't jog every day.

1. Michael/jog?
2. Sandra/play tennis?
3. Keith/play football?
4. Anna/do yoga?
5. Helen/swim?
6. Martin/run round the park?

3. Talk about people's routines
Look at page 55 and correct the information.
Vince starts work at 8.
No, he doesn't. He starts work at 8.30.

1. Vince starts work at 8.
2. Diana has lunch in a restaurant.
3. Joanne goes to bed at 10.
4. Paul gets up at 6 o'clock.
5. Vince reads the newspaper at breakfast.
6. Joanne watches TV after supper.

4. Talk about your family (Open exercise)
I've got three sisters. What about you?
I haven't got any sisters.

1. three sisters
2. two brothers
3. five children
4. a sister and a brother
5. a cat
6. a dog

5. Talk about the weather
What's the weather like in Mexico now?
It's very hot.

1. Mexico/very hot
2. London/raining
3. Madrid/quite nice
4. New York/very warm
5. Oslo/quite cold
6. Paris/lovely

Grammar

What	am / are / is	I / you they / he she	doing?

I'm We're They're He's She's	reading the paper. watching television. having breakfast.

What	do / does	you they / he she	do	on Monday evening(s)? on Sunday(s)? at the weekend? after supper? before supper?

I We They	go to evening classes. go swimming.
He She	goes swimming. watches TV.

What time When	do / does	you they / he she	get up? start work?

I They	get up at 8. start work at 9.
He She	gets up at 8. starts work at 9.

Have / Has	you they / he she	got any	brothers? sisters? children?

I We They / He She	haven't / hasn't	got any	brothers or sisters. children. daughters.

I've We've They've He's She's	got	a brother and a sister. two children. three sons.

This is	my his her our your their	son. daughter.

What's (What is) the weather like?	
It's	nice. hot. raining.

Isn't it	a lovely day? an awful day? hot (today)? cold (today)?	Yes, it's	beautiful. terrible.

Unit 8   At the Kennedys'

🔊 Dialogue: Part 1

DOUG: Hello! Come in! This is my wife, Liz. Liz, these are the people from Focus. Diana Trent and Paul Roberts.

LIZ: Hello. Nice to meet you. Was it far for you to come?

DIANA: No, I walked across the park. You're very near the park.

LIZ: Yes, we're lucky. I work in Kensington and I often cycle to work across the park.

PAUL: Oh, is it far?

LIZ: No, it only takes me about twenty-five minutes. I like the exercise. Doug's lazy. He always goes to work by underground.

DOUG: No, I don't. Not always.

LIZ: *(laughing)* No, you're right. You sometimes take a taxi! Come on, let's eat.

Are these true or false?
Doug and Liz live near the park.
Liz walks across the park to work.
Doug usually goes to work by underground.

Set 1   Journeys

1.	How do you get to work?	
I	go by	bus. train. underground. car.
	drive. walk. cycle.	

How far is it?	
It's about	5 miles. (8 kilometres)
How long does it take?	
It takes about twenty minutes.	

Work with your partner. Look at the chart. One of you takes the part of the people in the chart, like this:

How do you get to work, Doug?
I usually go by underground.
How far is it?
It's about . . . .

Name:	Doug	Liz	Paul	Diana
Method of transport:	underground	cycle	car	walk
Distance to work:	3 miles (5 kilometres)	2 miles (3½ kilometres)	5 miles (8 kilometres)	1 mile (1½ kilometres)
Time:	20 minutes	25 minutes	10 minutes	15 minutes

2. Talk and write about their journeys, like this:

Doug usually goes to work by underground. It's about 3 miles and it takes him about twenty minutes.

3. Ask your partner about his/her journey to work or school. Write about it in the same way.

4.   Do you ever cycle to work, Liz?
Yes, often.

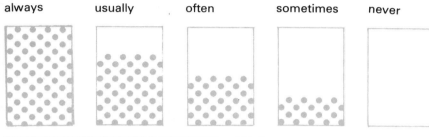

always   usually   often   sometimes   never

Name	cycle to work	late for work	take a taxi	work late in the evenings
Doug	never	sometimes	sometimes	always
Liz	often	never	never	often
Paul	sometimes	often	sometimes	never
Diana	never	sometimes	often	usually

In pairs, ask and answer questions, like this:

Do you ever cycle to work, Doug?
No, never.
Are you ever late for work?
Yes, sometimes.

Use both charts to write sentences about the people, like this:

Doug usually goes to work by underground, but he sometimes takes a taxi. He never cycles.
He's sometimes late for work. He always works late in the evenings.

Talk and write about yourself in the same way.

5.		Every			day. week.
How often do you go out?	About	once twice three times		a	month. year.

Ask and answer in pairs:

How often do you

go to the cinema?	go swimming?	travel abroad?
theatre?	on holiday?	see your parents?
hairdresser's?	to church?	buy bread?

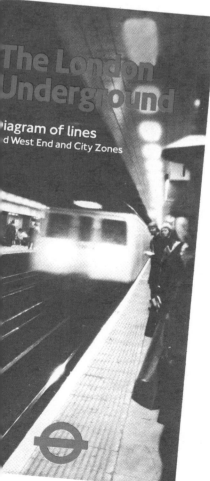

The London Underground

...iagram of lines
...d West End and City Zones

📼 Dialogue: Part 2

DIANA: It all looks delicious!
DOUG: Would you like chicken or beef, or both?
DIANA: I'd like beef, please.
DOUG: And would you like salad with it?
DIANA: Yes, please.
DOUG: What sort would you like?
DIANA: I don't know. What is there?
DOUG: There's potato salad, bean salad, green salad.
DIANA: I'd like some of each, please. Thanks.
DOUG: OK, Diana. Let's talk about your film. What's it about?

Answer:
What meat is there?
What salad is there?
What does Diana have?

SERVE YOURSELF! *all you can eat for 10$*

Salads
for your first course

Green Salad · Tomato Salad
Red Bean Salad · Potato Salad
Bread and Butter
DRESSINGS
French · Italian · Blue Cheese

Desserts
for your third course

Ice cream ~ Vanilla or Chocolate
Fresh fruit salad
Apple pie

Hot dishes
for your second course

MEAT AND FISH
Roast Chicken · Beef · Lamb · Pork
Fish in cheese sauce
VEGETABLES
Roast or Boiled potatoes
Beans · Carrots · Peas
Vegetable Pie

Drinks (extra)

Red or white wine (by the glass)
Beer or lager
Mineral water
Coca-cola

have a nice day!

Please pay at the checkout. Service is included

Set 2 Food and drink

You and a friend are having a birthday lunch in an American self-service restaurant. Look at the menu on page 62. Choose a few items from each course. Ask and answer like this:

A: Would you like a salad?
B: Yes, please.
A: Would you like tomato salad or green salad?
B: I'd like tomato salad, please.

A: What sort of salad would you like?
B: What is there?
A: There's green salad, tomato salad, red bean salad and potato salad.
B: I'd like potato salad, please.

Ask in the same way about:
1. dressings   3. desserts
2. hot dishes   4. drinks

Open dialogue
Look at the menu and talk to your friend in the restaurant.

FRIEND: Would you like a salad for your first course?
YOU: . . . .
FRIEND: What sort would you like?
YOU: . . . .
FRIEND: There's green salad, tomato salad, red bean salad and
        potato salad.
YOU: . . . .
FRIEND: Would you like some dressing with it?
YOU: . . . .
FRIEND: What about the second course? What would you like?
YOU: . . . .
FRIEND: Would you like roast or boiled potatoes with it?
YOU: . . . .
FRIEND: And what sort of vegetables would you like?
YOU: . . . .
FRIEND: Fine. And to drink?
YOU: . . . .
FRIEND: There's red or white wine, beer, lager, coke or mineral
        water.
YOU: . . . .
FRIEND: Mmm. That chicken was delicious. I think I'd like a dessert now.
        What is there?
YOU: . . . .
FRIEND: I'd like apple pie. What about you?
YOU: . . . .
FRIEND: Well, cheers! And happy birthday!

Roleplay
Work in groups of four.
One of you is the host/hostess. It is your birthday and you
    want to have a good meal.
One of you is on a diet.
One of you is vegetarian.
One of you is very hungry and thirsty.

Take a part each and choose your lunch together.

🔘 Dialogue: Part 3

PAUL: It's quite a big house. How many floors are there?

DOUG: Three altogether and a basement. There's the sitting room and the kitchen on the ground floor, three rooms on the next floor, and three on the top floor.

LIZ: And my study is in the basement.

DOUG: There's a small garden at the back, too.

PAUL: Well, it's a lovely house.

LIZ: Yes, we like it, too, but there's one thing . . .

DIANA: What's that?

LIZ: Too many stairs!

DOUG: The stairs!

Answer:
How many floors are there?
Does Paul like the house?
What don't Liz and Doug like about the house?

Set 3 House and home

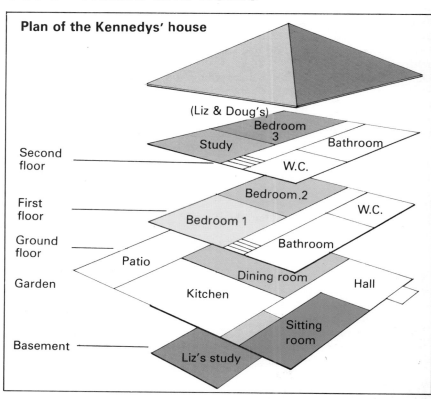

Plan of the Kennedys' house

(Liz & Doug's)

Bedroom 3

Study

Bathroom

W.C.

Second floor

Bedroom 2

First floor

Bedroom 1

W.C.

Ground floor

Bathroom

Garden

Patio

Dining room

Hall

Kitchen

Basement

Liz's study

Sitting room

1. How many floors are there?
   There are three altogether, and a basement.

Look at the plan of the Kennedys' house. Ask and answer in pairs, like this:
How many bedrooms are there?
      studies
      bathrooms
      toilets (W.C.)
      rooms (apart from the hall, the bathrooms and toilets)

2. Where's the kitchen? | Where are the toilets?
   It's on the ground floor. | There's one on the first floor
                            | and another on the second floor.

Look at the plan again and ask and answer about these rooms:
the kitchen   the dining room   Liz's study
the sitting room   Liz and Doug's   the other bedrooms
the bathrooms   bedroom

3. What colour is the study in the basement? It's brown.

Find the colours:
      black
      blue
      green
      orange
      red
      white
      yellow

Ask and answer questions about the colours in the different rooms.

4. Tell your partner about each floor of the Kennedys' house, like this:
      There's a big kitchen on the ground floor.

Talk and then write about the other floors of the house, like this:
      There's/There are . . .

Writing
Write two or three sentences about your home.

Reading

Gavin is a student from Cardiff College of Further Education. He is spending a year at the Sorbonne University in Paris. After a few weeks in Paris he wrote a letter to his friends at the college.

Paris,
21st October

Dear All,
I am writing this letter in my room and I can see the river Seine from my window. It's beautiful.
I am staying in a student hostel some miles from the centre of Paris. I've got a big room and I use it as a bedroom and a study and a sitting room! I share a big kitchen with the other students in the hostel. I sometimes cook here, but I usually have my meals at the University. The food there is good and quite cheap.
The University is about two stops from here on the Metro (the underground). It only takes ten minutes to get there, so that's easy. Most of the other students cycle, but I haven't got a cycle yet.
I'm enjoying myself very much. Paris is a fascinating city. I really like walking round the old parts. It's very different from Cardiff!
Do write if you have time,
All the best
Yours,
Gavin

Which is the right answer?

1. Gavin is studying in a) Cardiff at the moment.
                        b) Paris.
2. He is living a) in the centre of Paris.
               b) in the country.
               c) near the centre of Paris.
3. He has a) one room.
          b) two rooms.
          c) three rooms.
4. He a) sometimes eats at the hostel.
     b) never
     c) always
5. He usually a) walks to the University every morning.
             b) goes by underground.
             c) cycles.
6. He likes a) walking round the old parts of Paris.
           b) walking in the country.
           c) Cardiff.

Writing

Use Gavin's letter to help you to write a letter to a friend. Imagine you are staying at the Tower Hotel in London for a week's holiday. Use the questions below to help you plan your letter.

PARAGRAPH 1:	Where are you writing the letter?
	Where are you staying?
PARAGRAPH 2:	What can you see from your window?
	What is the hotel like?
	What is your hotel room like?
PARAGRAPH 3:	How far is the hotel from the West End?
	How do you get to the West End?
	How long does it take you?
PARAGRAPH 4:	Do you like London?
	What do you like doing most?

END THE LETTER LIKE THIS:
Please write if you have time.
All the best.
Yours,
(Your first name)

🔊 Listening

Lynette lives in Brighton. One place she likes to visit is the Brighton Pavilion. This beautiful building was once the summer house of the Prince Regent in the late eighteenth and early nineteenth century. Listen to Lynette and note down the rooms she talks about.

Oral exercises

1. Ask about rooms
You are in a friend's house or flat.
You want to find the bathroom.
Is this the bathroom?
No, the bathroom's over there.

1. bathroom/no, the bathroom's over there
2. toilet/yes, that's right
3. kitchen/yes, it is
4. the bedroom/no, it's the next one
5. dining room/no, it's next to the sitting room
6. sitting room/that's right

2. Talk about journeys
How far is it to work, Doug?
It's about 3 miles. It takes me twenty minutes.

1. Doug/3 miles/20 mins
2. Liz/2 miles/25 mins
3. Paul/5 miles/10 mins
4. Diana/1 mile/15 mins
5. Vince/10 miles/45 mins
6. Joanne/½ mile/5 mins

3. Answer about your routine (Open exercise)
Are you ever late for work?
(Yes, sometimes.)
Do you ever take a taxi?
(No, never.)

1. Are you ever late for work or school?
2. Do you ever take a taxi?
3. Do you ever walk to work or school?
4. Do you ever work at weekends?
5. Do you ever go home for lunch?
6. Do you ever travel in your job?

4. Answer about your life (Open exercise)
How often do you get up before seven?
(About once a week.)

1. How often do you get up before seven?
2. How often do you go to bed after midnight?
3. How often do you watch TV?
4. How often do you go to a concert?
5. How often do you buy a new record?

5. Offer a choice of food and drink
I'd like some salad.
Would you like some green salad or some tomato salad?
Some green salad, please.

1. some salad/green/tomato
2. some dressing/French/Italian
3. some meat/beef/chicken
4. some vegetables/beans/peas
5. some wine/white/red

Grammar

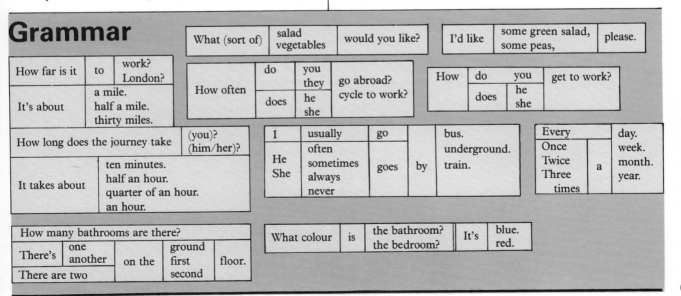

What (sort of)	salad vegetables	would you like?	I'd like	some green salad, some peas,	please.

How far is it	to	work? London?
It's about	a mile. half a mile. thirty miles.	

	do	you they	go abroad? cycle to work?
How often	does	he she	

How	do	you	get to work?
	does	he she	

How long does the journey take	(you)? (him/her)?
It takes about	ten minutes. half an hour. quarter of an hour. an hour.

I	usually	go		bus.
He She	often sometimes always never	goes	by	underground. train.

Every Once Twice Three times		a	day. week. month. year.

How many bathrooms are there?			
There's	one another	on the	ground first second	floor.
There are two				

What colour	is	the bathroom? the bedroom?	It's	blue. red.

Unit 9 | An evening out

Diana phones a friend, Judy Pattison.

JUDY: 5213. Hello.
DIANA: Hello. Is that Judy?
JUDY: Yes, speaking.
DIANA: Judy, it's Di here. Di Trent.
JUDY: Oh, hello Di! How are you?
DIANA: Fine, thanks. And you?
JUDY: Oh, very well. Where are you?
DIANA: I'm here in London. I'm at a video conference.
JUDY: How nice!

Set 1   Telephoning

	someone you know well	someone you don't know very well
1.	5213. Hello. Hello. Is that Judy? Yes, speaking. Judy, it's Di here. Di Trent. Oh, hello, Di! How are you?	5213. Hello. Hello. Is that Mrs Pattison? Yes, speaking. It's John Watson here, from Barclays Bank. Oh, hello, Mr Watson.

Judy is at home. These people telephone her. Practise the telephone conversations in pairs.

Sally Andrews — an old school friend
Mrs Rowe — an assistant at the film library
John Stamp — a friend from her old job
Martin Sloane — from the local newspaper

2.	5213. Hello. Oh, hello. Can I speak to Judy, please? It's Diana Trent here. I'm afraid she's out. Can I take a message? No, it's all right. I'll phone back later.

Work in pairs. Practise the conversation using the same names as in Exercise 1.

🔊 Dialogue: Part 2

JUDY: How long are you here?

DIANA: I leave on the 18th. But listen, are you free this evening?

JUDY: Yes, I am. Bob's in France until the end of May.

DIANA: Well, would you like to go out somewhere?

JUDY: Yes, I'd love to.

DIANA: Let's meet outside Leicester Square underground station at 6.

JUDY: Fine! See you then. Bye!

Set 2 Months and dates

1.	January February March April May June July August September October November December

Answer these questions about your country:
Which months are hot?
Which months are cold?
In which months does it rain a lot?
Which months are summer/winter/spring/autumn months?

2.		
1st first	11th eleventh	21st twenty-first
2nd second	12th twelfth	22nd twenty-second
3rd third	13th thirteenth	23rd twenty-third
4th fourth	14th fourteenth	24th twenty-fourth
5th fifth	15th fifteenth	25th twenty-fifth
6th sixth	16th sixteenth	26th twenty-sixth
7th seventh	17th seventeenth	27th twenty-seventh
8th eighth	18th eighteenth	28th twenty-eighth
9th ninth	19th nineteenth	29th twenty-ninth
10th tenth	20th twentieth	30th thirtieth

18th May (the eighteenth of May)

Answer:
When is your birthday? It's in *(month)*.
It's on *(date)*.
When is your teacher's birthday?
What date is it today/tomorrow?
What date was it yesterday?
When is the next public holiday?
When is the end of term?

spring

summer

autumn

winter

📼 Dialogue: Part 3

JUDY: Which film shall we see?
DIANA: There's nothing good on at the moment. Let's do something different. Would you like to go to a concert?
JUDY: Yes, I'd love to. Here's a good one. Mozart and Brahms. It's on at the Festival Hall. Shall we go to that?

DIANA: Fine! Do you want anything to eat now?
JUDY: No, I'm not very hungry.
DIANA: Well, let's go and have something to drink instead.
JUDY: I know a good place. It's quite expensive, but it's fun.

Answer:
Do Diana and Judy go to the cinema?
What do they do?
Where is it on?
What sort of music is it?
Are they hungry?
Do they go to a cheap place to have a drink?

Set 3   Invitations

1. Would you like to go out?
    Yes, I'd love to.

Work in pairs. Invite your partner to do the following:

come to lunch	go to a club	go dancing
come to my house	go for a walk	go swimming
play tennis	play cards	

2. You want to go to a pop concert one evening next week and you want someone to go with you. You are free on three evenings only. Decide which evenings. Go round the class, with your diary, and find someone to go to the pop concert with you.

Sun 16	Tues 18	Thurs 20	Sat 22
Mon 17	Wed 19	Fri 21	

Ask and answer, like this:
Are you free on Monday the 17th?
No. I'm afraid I'm not.
Well, are you free on Friday the 21st?
Yes, I am.
Oh good! I've got two tickets for . . . . Would you like to come with me?
Yes, I'd love to.

Set 4 Suggestions

> **1.** It's Diana's birthday next week. What shall we give her?
> Let's give her some roses.
> No, not flowers. Let's give her a record.

With a partner discuss what to give Paul, Vince and Joanne.
Choose from these presents:

a book
a sweater
a camera
a pen
a record
a T-shirt
a watch
a bag
some perfume
some aftershave

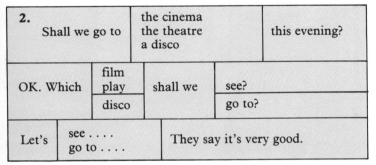

2.

Shall we go to	the cinema the theatre a disco	this evening?

OK. Which	film play	shall we	see?
	disco		go to?

Let's	see . . . . go to	They say it's very good.

DISCOS

★ **Hombre De Bahi** 78 Wells Street, W1 (580 2881) Oxford Circus tube. M/ship ring for details. Admission £3.50m&f. 9pm 3.30am Mon-Sat. Dress smart. Large West End disco – pool room, two bars and big dance floor. A good mid-week venue with party nights Tue and Thurs.

★ **Kereba** 63 Conduit Street, W1 (734 2187) Oxford Circus tube. M/ship £10m&f. Admission £3m, £2f. 9.30pm-3am. Dress casual but smart.

★ **Lazers** Salisbury Promenade, N8 (802 0303) Turnpike Lane tube. M/ship ring for details. Admission £1 membs, £1.50 guests weekdays; £1.50 membs, £2 guests w/ends. 9pm-2am Thurs, 9pm-3am Fri & Sat, 7pm-12am Sun. Dress casual but smart.

THEATRE

★ **Greenwich** Crooms Hill, SE10 (858 7755) Greenwich BR. (S) 'Another Country' by Julian Mitchell, directed by Stuart Burge. New play set in English public school in the 1930s. 7.45; Sat mats 2.30. £2-£5. (Ends Dec 12).

★ **Haymarket** SW1 (930 9832) Piccadilly Circus tube. From Tue: 'An Evening with Dave Allen' 8.00. £3.50-£7.50.

★ **Her Majesty's** Haymarket, SW1 (930 6606) Piccadilly Circus tube. 'Amadeus' by Peter Shaffer, directed by Peter Hall with Frank Finlay, Richard O'Callaghan, Morag Hood. National Theatre Production. 8.00; Sat mat 3.00. (From Mon Nov 7, 7.30). £3-£7.50. (Runs 2½ hours).

★ **London Palladium** Argyll St, W1 (437 7373) Oxford Circus tube. 'Barnum' with music by Cy Coleman, lyrics by Michael Stewart, book by Mark Bramble. London production of the American musical with Michael Crawford. Mon-Sat 7.30; Wed, Sat mats 2.45. £2.50-£8.50. (Runs 2¼ hours).

Look at the advertisements for films, plays and discos.
Choose:

a film you want to see
a play or musical you want to see
a disco you want to go to

Make conversations with your partner about your evening out.

📼 Dialogue: Part 4

DIANA: Did you enjoy it?
JUDY: Yes, I did. Did you?
DIANA: Yes. It was all right. But I didn't like the Brahms very much, I'm afraid.
JUDY: Really? Why?
DIANA: It was too slow.
JUDY: Oh, I liked it.
DIANA: Judy, I'm a bit tired. I think I need some fresh air. I think I'll walk back to the hotel.

Are these true or false?
Judy enjoyed the concert.
Diana also enjoyed the concert very much.
Diana liked the Brahms because it was slow.
Judy is tired after the concert.

Set 5 Opinions

1.
Did you enjoy the concert?
Yes, I did. Did you?
It was all right. I liked the Mozart, but I didn't like the Brahms very much.

Talk about the following in the same way:
the meal/chicken/dessert
the concert/the first group/the other groups
the holiday/the hotel/the town
the film *Reds*/Diane Keaton/Warren Beatty

2.
Did you like the Brahms?
No, I didn't. Not very much.
Really? Why not?
It was too slow.

Ask and answer in pairs about the following:
the film/long   music/loud   book/sad
Stockholm/cold   sightseeing/trip/fast

🔊 Open dialogue

It is Saturday evening. You meet Paul.

PAUL: Hello. Isn't it a beautiful evening?
YOU: . . . .
PAUL: Would you like to do something?
YOU: . . . .
PAUL: OK. What's the date today?
YOU: . . . .
PAUL: Right. Let's look in the paper and see what's on.
    What shall we do?
YOU: . . . .
PAUL: OK. Shall I meet you at your house?
YOU: . . . .
PAUL: What's the address?
YOU: . . . .
PAUL: What time shall I come?
YOU: . . . .
PAUL: Fine! I'll see you then. Bye!
YOU: . . . .

Roleplay

Choose a film, play or disco to go to. Telephone a friend.
Ask if he/she is free on . . . . (*name a date*)
Invite him/her to do something.
Arrange when to meet.
        where to meet.
        where to go after the film/play/disco/restaurant.

First look at Diana and Judy's telephone conversation on page 68.
Start your conversation in the same way.

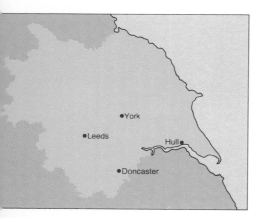

Reading

Sharon lives in Scawsby, in Yorkshire. She hates Scawsby.
'There's nothing to do in the evenings,' says Sharon. 'It's very boring.'

Scawsby is a few miles from a big town called Doncaster. It takes about twenty minutes by bus to get from Scawsby to Doncaster. But Sharon doesn't like Doncaster because there isn't anything to do there either. 'I go there about once a week, but nothing exciting ever happens there. I want to live in London. In London there's always something interesting to do, and somewhere exciting to go. There's always someone new to meet.'

Sharon finished school in July on her sixteenth birthday. She starts her first job in a shoe factory outside Scawsby in September. She's looking forward to it very much. 'I want to work because I need my own money. But on my seventeenth birthday I want to go to London.'

Write questions for these answers:
1. In Scawsby in Yorkshire.
2. No, she doesn't. She hates it.
3. Because there isn't anything to do in the evening.
4. A few miles.
5. About twenty minutes.
6. In London.
7. Because there's always something interesting to do there.
8. In July.
9. In September.
10. In a shoe factory.
11. Yes, she is.
12. She wants to go to London.

🔊 Listening

Liz Kennedy telephones a friend, Mary, about an invitation. Listen to them talking about it and fill in the missing information from the invitation card.

Writing

Use the poster to complete this letter.

Adam and Diana Black would like you to come to a

....

on .... *at* .... *London* W1
at ....
RSVP
7 The Boltons, London SW7

Dear Malcolm,
I've ____ two ____ for ____ on ____.
Are you ____ that evening? Would
____ ____ ____ ____ come ____ me?
They say ____ ____ ____.
Please ____ or ____ and tell me if you
can ____.
Yours
Dave.

Now write a letter like this to one of your friends and invite him/her to do something with you one evening next week.

Oral exercises

1. Say who you are on the telephone
2314. Hello. Sally speaking.
Oh, hello, Sally. It's Di here.

1. 2314/Sally
2. 3406/Denis
3. 4413/Robert
4. 1216/Delia
5. 9378/Ann
6. 6514/John

2. Talk about arrangements
Are you free on the 9th?
No, not on the 9th, I'm afraid.

1. 9th
2. 1st
3. 3rd
4. 5th
5. 2nd
6. 28th

3. Make suggestions(1)
What shall we do?
Shall we go to the theatre?
Yes, let's.

1. National Theatre: *Othello*
2. Cinecenta: *Superman III*
3. Festival Hall: Mozart Clarinet Quintet
4. The Embassy: Disco dancing
5. La Cuisine: French food
6. BBC1: *Dallas*

4. Make suggestions (2)
What shall we give Paul for his birthday?
Let's give him a T-shirt.

1. Paul/T-shirt
2. Diana/pen
3. my mother/some flowers
4. my brother/a book about cars
5. the children/a Walt Disney video cassette
6. my parents/some theatre tickets

5. Ask and talk about availability
Is there anything to drink?
I'm afraid there isn't anything. There's nothing to drink at all.

1. drink
2. eat
3. read
4. watch on television
5. listen to on the radio

Grammar

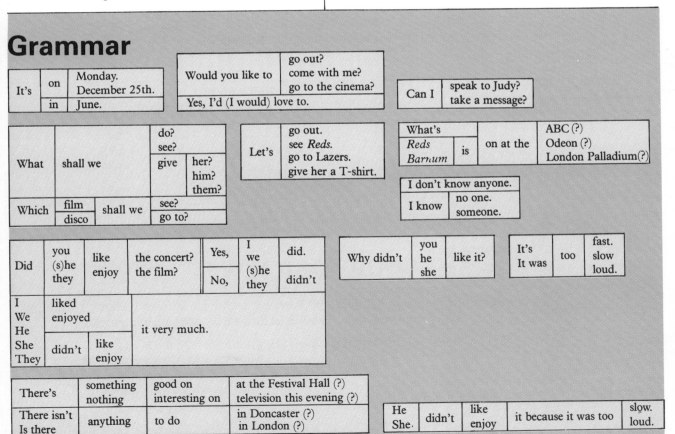

75

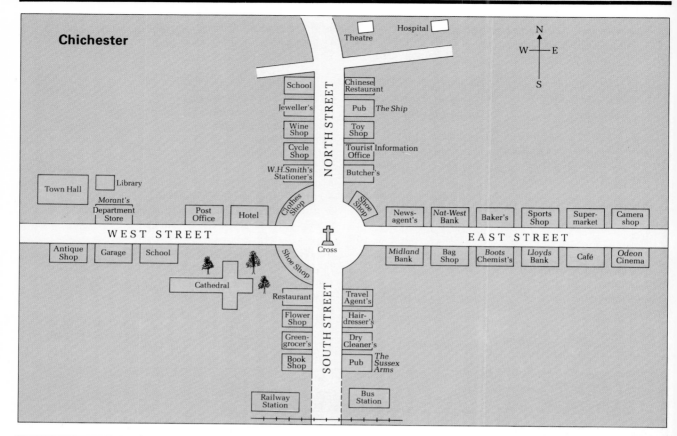

Chichester

Map labels:
- Theatre
- Hospital
- N W E S (compass)
- School
- Chinese Restaurant
- Jeweller's
- Pub — The Ship
- Wine Shop
- Toy Shop
- Cycle Shop
- Tourist Information Office
- W.H.Smith's Stationer's
- Butcher's
- NORTH STREET
- Town Hall
- Library
- Morant's Department Store
- Post Office
- Hotel
- Clothes Shop
- Shoe Shop
- News-agent's
- Nat-West Bank
- Baker's
- Sports Shop
- Super-market
- Camera shop
- WEST STREET
- EAST STREET
- Cross
- Antique Shop
- Garage
- School
- Cathedral
- Shoe Shop
- Restaurant
- Midland Bank
- Bag Shop
- Boots Chemist's
- Lloyds Bank
- Café
- Odeon Cinema
- Travel Agent's
- Flower Shop
- Hair-dresser's
- Greengrocer's
- Dry Cleaner's
- Book Shop
- Pub — The Sussex Arms
- SOUTH STREET
- Railway Station
- Bus Station

TOURIST INFORMATION:

Banks:	Midland	East Street
	National Westminster	Open weekdays
	Lloyds	9.30-3.30
Pubs:	The Ship	North Street
	The Sussex Arms	South Street
		open
		10.30-2.30
		5.30-11.00
Department Store:	Morant's	West Street
		Open 9-5.30
		Early closing
		Monday 1p.m.

Bus 268 and 269

Chichester	Waterbeach (Nr. Goodwood House)
Dep.	Arr.
10.10	10.25
12.10	12.25
14.10	14.25
16.10	16.25
18.10	18.25

*The same bus returns to Chichester 10 mins after arrival in Waterbeach

GOODWOOD HOUSE

Goodwood House, home of the Dukes of Richmond since 1697, centre of the 12,000 acre estate and all its many activities, contains the famous collections of furniture, porcelain and paintings.

GOODWOOD HOUSE: Traditional Open Days:
Sundays and Mondays from May to mid-October (except horse event days). Also Tuesdays, Wednesdays and Thursdays in August.

The State Apartments are open 2 p.m. to 5 p.m. Tea available in the House. Parties must book tea in advance.

CHICHESTER FESTIVAL THEATRE

...the theatre for all seasons........

Seating plan

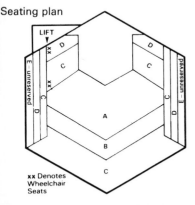

xx Denotes Wheelchair Seats

CHICHESTER FESTIVAL THEATRE

May		The Northern Ballet's
Mon	3	delightful new
Tues	4	production of
Wed	5	**A Midsummer Night's**
Thur	6	**Dream.** Nightly at 7.30,
Fri	7	with 2.30 matinees on
Sat	8	Thursday and
		Saturday.

Prices: A £8, B £6, C £4, D £3, E £2

Jason's Bistro

CHICHESTER

In South Street, you can enjoy reasonably priced, original food, in an informal atmosphere with friendly service.
LUNCHEONS 12.00- 2.00
DINNERS 7.30-11.30 (last orders)
MONDAY TO SATURDAY
- FULLY LICENSED
For Reservations, telephone:
Chichester 783158
Car park available at back of restaurant for evening diners.
DIRECTIONS
Drive south on ring road to railway/bus station, head up South Street and the Bistro is on the left, at the end of the street.

1. Work with a partner. One of you is staying in Chichester, at the hotel in West Street. The other person is a Tourist Information Officer. Only he/she can see the information on these pages.

It is 9.00 a.m. on Monday, May 3rd. You want some information about Chichester. You want to plan your day. You want to:
1. see something interesting.
2. do something interesting.
3. eat somewhere afterwards.
4. go shopping.

Ask your partner:
1. if there is anything interesting to see outside Chichester.
   if it is open on Mondays.
   what time it opens and closes.
   how you get there.
   how often the buses leave Chichester for Goodwood.
   how long the journey takes.
   if there is a bus from Chichester at about . . . o'clock.
2. if there is anything interesting on at the Festival Theatre.
   what time it starts.
   how much the tickets are.
   for two tickets at a price you want to pay.
3. if there is a good restaurant in Chichester.
   where it is.
   if it is open on Monday evenings.
   what time it closes.
4. if there is a department store in Chichester.
   where it is.
   if it is open on Mondays.
   what time it closes.
   where you can buy stamps, a newspaper, a film for your camera and some new shoes.

Thank the person and leave.

Telephone a friend and invite him or her to do one of the things you have planned to do in Chichester. Arrange when and where to meet.

2. GAME: Where am I?
Look at the plan of the town on page 76. Choose a place to be, for example, in the theatre. Your partner must try to guess where you are. 'Are you in East Street?' etc.

📼 Listening

1. A man is directing a woman in the street. The woman is outside the bus station in Chichester. Follow the directions on the map as you listen and note down where the woman wants to go.
2. Listen to some children talking. Note down what things they like doing at school. Choose from the following:

> reading   writing   mathematics   acting   singing   watching TV
> counting   playing   spelling   painting   doing gym   dancing

Do you know any children? What do they like doing at school? Write a few sentences.

3. Listen to Karen talking about her family. Complete the family tree below and the ages of the children.

Lynne (mother)	(father)

	Karen aged 7		

Write about Karen's family, like this:
Karen's mother is called . . . . . and her father . . . . .
Karen has three . . . . . One is called . . . . . and is . . . . . years old.
Another is . . . . .

Now write about a family you know.

4. Puzzle it out!
Listen to these seven short scenes and write in the spaces below the name of the place or shop the people are in. When you have the names of all seven places, you will have the name of an 8th shop.

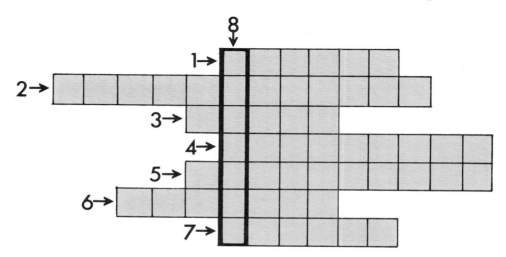

Reading

A DAY IN THE LIFE OF PETER MAXWELL
Peter Maxwell is unemployed. He is 24.

'I usually get up at about eight o'clock. Then I have breakfast — coffee or tea, and some toast. After this I go down to the library and read the papers. There are a lot of us at the library. We never say we're unemployed but we know. I look at all the possible jobs in the papers (this takes about a minute!), I read the sports and the arts pages, and soon it's time for lunch so I go off down to the shops for bread, milk, fresh vegetables and 25 pence worth of cheese. I like shopping, and I like cooking now, too. On the way back from the shops I buy a local paper and look at the job advertisements over lunch (soup and bread and butter).

After 'lunch' on Mondays and Wednesdays I go to a carpentry class. These classes are free for unemployed people. It's important to do a lot of things when you're unemployed. You need a routine for the day. On the other days of the week I go for walks if the weather's all right, or I read.

At about six o'clock I start preparing the Big Meal of the day. I take a lot of time over this. It's usually vegetables and cheese, or sometimes spaghetti bolognaise. After supper my wife and I read, or play chess. Every Friday we go to a pub, or to the cinema. I don't watch TV much. Usually at 10.30 we turn off the heater and go to bed.'

1. Write the questions for these answers:

1. Have you . . .?   No, I haven't. I'm unemployed.
2. What time . . .?   At eight o' clock.
3. What . . .?   Coffee or tea, and toast.
4. Where . . .?   To the library.
5. Why. . .?   Because I want to read the papers.
6. Which parts . . .? The job advertisements, the sports and arts pages.
7. What . . .?   I go shopping and I buy a local paper.
8. What . . .?   Usually I have soup and bread and butter.
9. What . . .?   I go to a carpentry class.
10. When . . .?   On Monday and Wednesday afternoons.
11. What . . .?   I go for a walk or read.
12. When . . .?   At about six.
13. What . . .?   Talk, play games or read.
14. Do . . .?   No, not much.
15. When . . .?   At about 10.30.

2. In pairs, roleplay an interview using the questions and answers above.

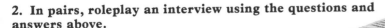

Reading for information

1. Look at the cinema advertisements and answer the questions:
How many films are showing at the Classic, Oxford Street?
How many films are showing at the Classic in the Haymarket?
How many are Walt Disney films?
How many times can you see *Time Bandits* in one day?
How many cinemas have Late Shows?

2. Answer with a time or times:
When is the first programme for *Clash of the Titans?*
When is the last programme for *Herbie Goes Bananas?*
When is the first programme for *Excalibur* on Sunday?
When do the Late Shows start?
When is the last programme for *The Great Muppet Caper* on Thursday?

3. Look at the advertisement for the river cruise and answer the questions:
Where can you buy a ticket for the river cruise?
What time does the cruise start and finish?
Which cathedrals does the launch pass?
How many bridges does the launch go under, between the start of
   the cruise and the Tower of London?
Which is the nearest underground station?
How much are tickets for children?

4. Plan a day out
1. You work in Oxford Street. You finish work at 5.30 p.m.
   You want to see a film, but you must be home before 9 p.m.
   Which film can you see?
2. You are entertaining a 12 year-old child in London for the afternoon
   and evening. You want to see a film and go on the river cruise. It takes
   about half an hour to travel to Westminster by underground from
   Piccadilly Circus and Tottenham Court Road underground stations.
   Work out your programme.

5. Use the advertisement to complete the letter.

HADLEY COMMON
Barnet, Herts. Detached
modern house, 3 bedrooms,
bathroom, 2 reception
rooms, kitchen/breakfast
room. Garage. Fully
furnished. £100 p.w. inc.
Taylor and Clegg.

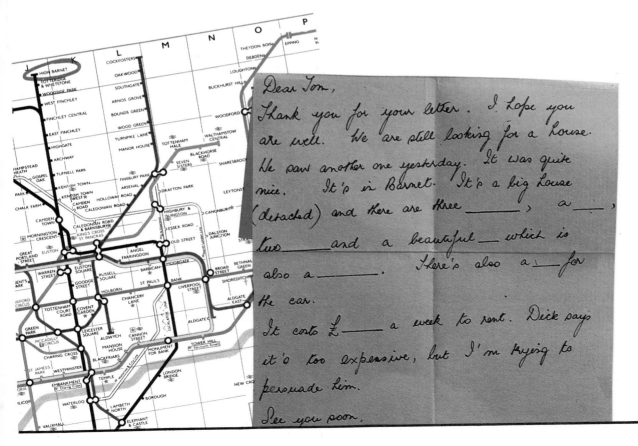

Dear Jon,

Thank you for your letter. I hope you are well. We are still looking for a house. We saw another one yesterday. It was quite nice. It's in Barnet. It's a big house (detached) and there are three _____, a _____, two _____ and a beautiful _____ which is also a _____. There's also a _____ for the car.

It costs £_____ a week to rent. Dick says it's too expensive, but I'm trying to persuade him.

See you soon,

Language focus

1. Which is correct, a, b or c?

1. A: a) Is there a post office near here?
       b) Is it a post office?
       c) Is the post office closed?
  B: Yes, there's one over there.

2. The performance a) starts   at 6.
                 b) start
                 c) it starts

3. Were you here last night? a) Yes, they were.
                            b) Yes, I was.
                            c) Yes, I am.

4. What's he doing? a) He's doing it.
                 b) He does exercises.
                 c) He's doing exercises.

5. a) He does always exercises in the morning.
  b) Always he does exercises
  c) He always does exercises

6. a) What does the weather like in New York?
  b) What's the weather like in New York?
  c) How is the weather like in New York?

7. A: a) Would you like some potatoes?
       b) Do you like potatoes?
       c) You like potatoes!
  B: Yes, I'd love some.

8. I haven't got a) some milk.
               b) no
               c) any

9. Let's meet a) in Wednesday afternoon.
            b) on Wednesday afternoon.
            c) on the afternoon of Wednesday.

2. Fill in the right form of the verbs in brackets:

(be)   ANN: Hello . . . . . that Jackie?
(speak) J: Yes, ...
(be)   A: Jackie, this . . . . . Ann. Listen, ... you free on January 21st?
(be)   J: You mean on Saturday? Yes, I . . . . . Why?
(get)   A: Well, I've . . . . tickets for the Haircut 100 concert at the Hammersmith Odeon.
(like)   . . . . . you . . . . . to come?
(love)   J: Yes, I . . . . to.
(like)   I . . . . . Haircut 100. What time
(start)   . . . . . the show. . . . .?
(meet)   A: At 7.30. . . . . . we . . . . . outside the Odeon?
(let/meet) J: No, ... at my house first. There
(be)   . . . . . always so many people outside the Odeon.
    A: OK. I'll see you at your house at about 7 on Saturday then.

3. Complete the conversation. You are in a restaurant with a friend.

WAITER: . . . .
FRIEND: I'd like a steak and a salad, please.
WAITER: And you, sir?
YOU: . . . .
WAITER: Yes. One steak and salad, and one roast beef with roast potatoes and peas.
FRIEND: Mmm. This steak is good. Is your beef all right?
YOU: . . . .
FRIEND: Oh good. By the way, ...
YOU: Warren Beatty? He's all right.
FRIEND: Well, there's a good film on at the ABC cinema with Warren Beatty in it. It's called *Reds*. Would you like to see it?
YOU: . . . .
FRIEND: Oh, good.
YOU: . . . .
FRIEND: I think it starts at 8.30.
YOU: Well, let's go then.
FRIEND: Waiter! Can I have the bill, please? Thank you.
YOU: . . . .?
FRIEND: £5 each.
YOU: OK. Here's my money.

4. Put these sentences in the right order:

A DAY IN THE LIFE OF PETER GIBBS.

1. Then he goes to work.
2. Here is a typical day for Peter.
3. He usually has lunch in the office canteen.
4. He goes to bed at about 11.30.
5. Peter Gibbs is a systems analyst.
6. After supper he usually reads the paper and watches TV or sees his girlfriend.
7. He works for a company in Swindon, a big town in the south of England.
8. He goes to work by car.
9. He finishes work at 5.30.
10. He starts work at 9 o'clock.
11. He gets up at 7 o'clock, reads the paper and has breakfast.
12. Then he goes home and has supper.
13. He sometimes goes swimming or plays squash.
14. In the summer he starts work at 8 o'clock.

Write a paragraph about Peter Gibbs, and then write a similar one about someone you know well.

5. In the puzzle below, find:

4 colours	4 shops or buildings
4 rooms of the house	4 family relations

You may use the same letter more than once. Words can read from left to right, right to left, top to bottom and bottom to top. For example:

Shops or buildings   *Family relations*
bank   sister

P	Q	D	T	K	N	A	B	P	S
R	M	A	C	I	N	E	M	A	U
E	L	U	Z	T	N	O	Q	S	V
C	F	G	X	C	E	N	M	I	L
I	B	H	C	H	E	M	I	S	T
F	A	T	H	E	R	B	H	T	K
F	C	E	A	N	G	E	H	E	J
O	D	R	L	C	F	D	E	R	P
T	O	I	L	E	T	R	I	L	O
S	J	O	Q	B	R	O	W	N	B
O	K	L	S	T	W	O	X	O	D
B	L	U	E	V	Z	M	M	S	G

Unit 11 Shopping

🔊 **Dialogue: Part 1** ⬜

PAUL: What are you doing this afternoon, Joanne? Are you going to the conference?

JOANNE: No, I'm not. But Vince is going. I'm going shopping. What about you?

PAUL: I don't know. Diana's in Cambridge. She's seeing some people about a film.

JOANNE: Oh. How long is she staying there?

PAUL: Just for the day. She's coming back this evening.

JOANNE: Well, let's go shopping together.

PAUL: That's a good idea. I need some new jeans.

Answer:
Who is going to the conference?
What is Joanne doing in the afternoon?
What is Diana doing in Cambridge?
How long is she staying there?
When is she coming back?
What does Paul want to buy?

Set 1 Plans for the near future

1. What	are you		doing this afternoon?	I'm	going	to	the conference. Cambridge.
	is	he she		He's She's			shopping.

Are you		to	the conference this afternoon? Cambridge?	Yes,	I am. he/she is.
Is	he she	going	shopping?	No,	I'm not. he/she isn't.

Monday 17th		
Name	A.M.	P.M.
JOANNE	Conference	shopping
VINCE	conference	conference
DIANA	Cambridge	Cambridge
PAUL	Conference	sightseeing

In pairs, ask and answer about each person's plans for the afternoon, like this:

> What are you doing this afternoon, Joanne? Are you going to the conference?
> No, I'm not. I'm going shopping.

2. Now ask and answer about the plans, like this:

> What's Joanne doing this afternoon? Is she going to the conference?
> No, she isn't. She's going shopping.

3. Doug Kennedy is talking to a friend at work:

DOUG: Where are you going for your holidays this year?

KIM: I'm going to Antigua.

DOUG: How marvellous! Where are you staying?

KIM: At a hotel called Half Moon Bay.

DOUG: How long are you staying?

KIM: For a fortnight.

DOUG: How lovely! When are you leaving?

KIM: On July 2nd.

DOUG: Well, have a nice time and bring me back a coconut!

Look at the holiday chart. Choose a place, a hotel and a date for your own holiday. In pairs, roleplay a similar conversation to the one above.

Destination	Hotel	Available departure dates
ANTIGUA	Half Moon Bay	April 30/July 2
BARBADOS	Cobblers Cove, Sandy Lane	May 30/July 11 May 2/October 31
KENYA	Bamburi Beach, Nyali Beach	April 26/July 12 May 3/July 29
MALAYSIA	Golden Sands, Rasa Sayang	May 8/October 2 May 8/July 31 & Sept 4/Oct 2
MAURITIUS	La Pirogue	April 27/June 29 & August 31/Nov 2
ST. LUCIA	Cariblue	April 26/June 28 & August 30/Oct 25
SEYCHELLES	The Reef	April 26/July 12 & August 23/Dec 13
TOBAGO	Mount Irvine, Turtle Beach	March 28/December 19 April 25/June 27 & October 3/31

Note: all holidays are for one, two or three weeks.

4.	this in the tomorrow on Tuesday		morning. afternoon. evening.
We're leaving	on		May 23rd. Saturday.
	at		10 a.m. lunchtime.
	next		week. Saturday.

Vince is staying in London after the conference. His wife, Kelly, and his children, are coming to London to join him for a fortnight's holiday. Look at Vince's diary for the next two weeks. Vince is talking to Diana about their plans. It is Monday, May 17th. Complete Vince's part of the conversation:

DIANA: When are your family arriving, Vince?
VINCE: . . . .
DIANA: Oh, are they? Are they going sightseeing in London?
VINCE: . . . .
DIANA: Oh, that's good. Those tours are quite good, I think. Are you going on any trips outside London?
VINCE: . . . .
DIANA: To Scotland! How lovely! When?
VINCE: . . . .
DIANA: How are you travelling?
VINCE: . . . .
DIANA: And how long are you staying there?
VINCE: . . . .
DIANA: Great! And then are you staying the rest of the time in London?
VINCE: . . . .
DIANA: To Stratford! How are you getting there? By train?
VINCE: . . . .
DIANA: That's a good idea. And have you got tickets for the theatre?
VINCE: . . . .
DIANA: They say it's very good. And you must see the musical *Cats*, too. It's marvellous!
VINCE: . . . .
DIANA: Oh, are you? When are you going back to the States?
VINCE: . . . .
DIANA: Well, enjoy your stay. It sounds fun.

5. Ask a few people in your class what they are doing
— this evening
— tomorrow
— next weekend
— next holidays

Tell them about your plans, too.

MAY 1983

Mon	17	
Tue	18	Conference ends. Meet Kelly and the kids Heathrow 8.p.m.
Wed	19	
Thu	20	10 a.m. Coach tour of London (Kelly and the kids)
Fri	21	Theatre 'Cats'
Sat	22	
Sun	23	9.30 p.m. EUSTON STATION Night train to Scotland
Mon	24	Scotland
Tue	25	Scotland / p.m. Back to London
Wed	26	Rent a car Stratford-upon Avon Theatre - A Midsummer Nights Dream
Thu	27	Stratford / Back to London
Fri	28	Dinner at Simpson's with Joanne
Sat	29	10. a.m. Leave Pan-am 125 Heathrow Airport
Sun	30	

📼 Dialogue: Part 2

JOANNE: What lovely sweaters!
GIRL: Can I help you?
JOANNE: Yes. Can I have a look at those sweaters?
GIRL: Yes, of course.
JOANNE: They're nice. Can I try a black one on?
GIRL: Certainly. What size are you?
JOANNE: Size 12, I think.

GIRL: Then you want a Medium. They come in Small, Medium and Large.
Joanne tries on a sweater.
JOANNE: It's nice, but it's a bit big. Can you give me a Small size please?
GIRL: Certainly. Here you are.
JOANNE: What do you think, Paul?
PAUL: It suits you.
JOANNE: I think I'll have it. How much does it cost?

GIRL: £19.95.
JOANNE: Can I pay by American Express?
GIRL: Yes, of course.

Answer:
What size is Joanne?
What does she try on?
How much does the sweater cost?
How does she pay for it?

Clothes sizes

GENERAL CLOTHES SIZES (including chest/hip measurements)

GB	8	10	12	14	16	18	20	22	24	26
USA	6	8	10	12	14	16	18	20	22	24
Europe	36	38	40	42	44	46	48	50	52	54
ins	30/32	32/34	34/36	36/38	38/40	40/42	42/44	44/46	46/48	48/50
cms	76/81	81/86	86/91	91/97	97/102	102/107	107/112	112/117	117/122	122/127

SHIRTS:
Collar measurements

GB/USA (ins)	14	14½	15	15½	16	16½	17	17½
Europe (cms)	36	37	38	39	40	41	42	43

SHOES:

GB		3	3½	4	4½	5	5½	6	6½	7	7½	8	8½	9
USA	4½	5		5½	6		6½	7		7½	8		8½	9	9½	10	10½
Europe	36			37		38			39		40			41		42

Set 2 Shopping for clothes

1. In pairs, use the list of clothes and accessories below to identify all the items you can see.

coat	skirt	shirt	jacket	tie
hat	sweater	dress	trousers	boot
T-shirt	bag	shoes	jeans	

2. What a	lovely smart	sweater! hat!	Can I have a look at	it?
What	nice pretty	sweaters! jeans!		them?

In pairs, use the language box to admire, and to ask to look at, the clothes and accessories.

3.	Can I try a sweater/some jeans on?
	Certainly. What size are you?
	Size 12, I think.
	Here you are. This is/These are size 12.
	It's/They're nice, but it's/they're a bit big/small/tight.
	Can you give me a size 10/14?

Choose three or four more items of clothing you want, and ask to try them on. Find your correct (GB) size from the chart of Clothes Sizes on page 87. Work in pairs. Take turns to play the part of the customer and the assistant.

4. How would you like to pay?
I'll pay cash.
Can I pay by │ credit card? (American Express etc.)
│ cheque?
│ travellers cheque?
Yes, of course/certainly.

In pairs, practise asking how you can pay for your goods.

Roleplay

One of you is the assistant in a clothes boutique, the other is the customer. The customer wants to buy some new clothes for a holiday in New York. Follow the guide for the customer below.

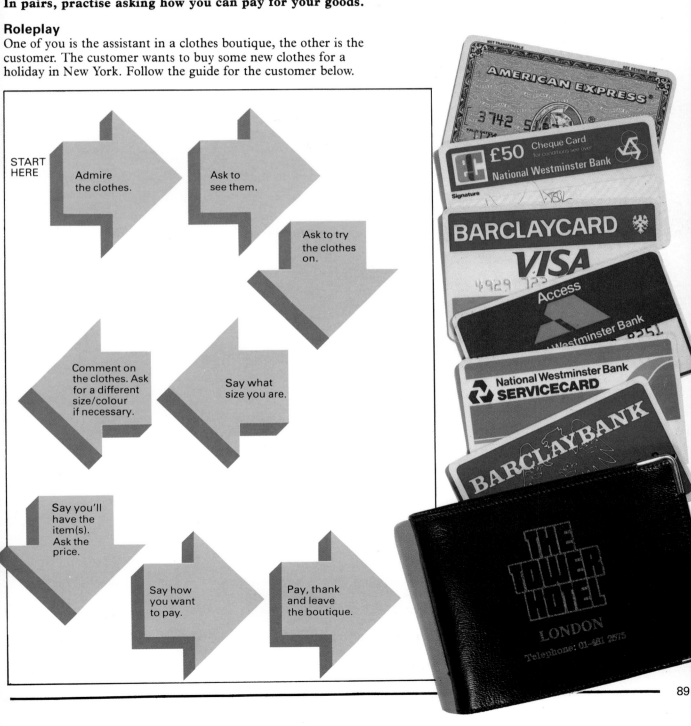

🔊 Listening

Joy is trying to arrange a date for a business meeting with Liz Kennedy.
Listen and answer these questions:

When is she going to Oxford?
How long is she staying there?
When is she having her parents to dinner?
When are she and Doug going to the theatre?
When is she seeing a business contact from Paris?
When can they meet?

Reading

This is a letter to Diana from her friend, Sarah:

Dear Diana,
    I'm writing this on Copacabana beach.
The children are swimming and Robert is learning
to surf. The weather is very hot! Tomorrow morning
we're going up the Sugarloaf Mountain and in the
afternoon I'm going shopping. I need some new
summer dresses. After two weeks here, I'm size 14!
Rio de Janeiro is marvellous and we're all
enjoying it here.
    We're meeting Robert's new boss in a smart
restaurant in Ipanema this evening. He started
the new job last Monday, and he's really pleased
with it. Write soon with all your news.
                            Love,
                        Sarah and the family.

P.S. Can you send me your sister's address?

Ask and answer:

Where are Sarah and the family living now?
Do they like it there?
What's the weather like?
Where is she writing the letter?
Where are Robert and the children?
What are they doing this evening?
What are they doing tomorrow morning?
What is she doing tomorrow afternoon?
When did Robert start his new job?
Does he like it?

Writing

Look at Vince's diary again on page 86. It is Monday. Complete the letter
on the left from Vince to his sister, telling her about some of his plans for
the next two weeks. End the letter like this:

We are looking forward to seeing you on Sunday.

Love from Vince.

THE TOWER HOTEL

Monday 17th May.
Dear Shirley,
    Everything is going just
fine here! Kelly and the kids
are arriving

St. Katharine's Way, London E1 9LD
Telephone: 01-481 2575
Cables: Towerhotel London E1
Telex: 885934

Oral exercises

1. Ask about plans

Joanne isn't going to the conference.
Oh, is she going shopping?
Yes, she is.
Vince and Kelly aren't going to a concert.
Oh, are they going to the theatre?
Yes, they are.

1. Joanne/not the conference/shopping?
2. Vince and Kelly/not a concert/the theatre?
3. Diana/not the conference/Cambridge?
4. Vince/not shopping/the conference?
5. Vince and his family/not Cambridge/Stratford?
6. Vince and his family/not by train to Stratford/by car?

2. Talk about plans (Open exercise)

Talk to Paul about your plans for the week.
What are you doing this evening?
I'm staying at home.
What are you doing tomorrow?
I'm coming to class.

1. What are you doing this evening?
2. What are you doing tomorrow?
3. What are you doing tomorrow evening?
4. What about Saturday? What are you doing then?
5. What are you doing on Sunday?
6. What are you doing in the summer holidays?

3. Ask permission in a shop (1)

We've got lots of T-shirts.
Can I have a look at them, please?
Yes, certainly.
This is a good camera.
Can I have a look at it, please?
Yes, certainly.

1. We've got lots of T-shirts.
2. This is a good camera.
3. We have very nice Italian shoes.
4. This is a French handbag.
5. We've got some new designer jeans.
6. This tie is from Yves St. Laurent.

4. Ask permission in a shop (2)

Do you like this sweater?
Yes. Can I try it on, please?
Yes, of course.
These jeans are your size.
Yes. Can I try them on, please?
Yes, of course.

1. Do you like this sweater?
2. These jeans are your size.
3. These ski boots are very good.
4. This jacket is very nice.
5. Do you like these shoes?
6. These trousers are American. They're very smart.

Grammar

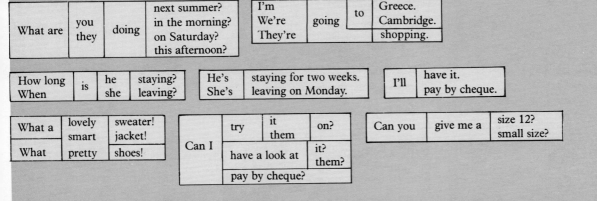

What are	you they	doing	next summer? in the morning? on Saturday? this afternoon?	I'm We're They're	going	to	Greece. Cambridge. shopping.

How long When	is	he she	staying? leaving?	He's She's	staying for two weeks. leaving on Monday.	I'll	have it. pay by cheque.

What a What	lovely smart pretty	sweater! jacket! shoes!	Can I	try have a look at pay by cheque?	it them it? them?	on?	Can you	give me a	size 12? small size?

🔊 Dialogue: Part 1

MAN: Jason, don't do that! It's dangerous.

JASON: No, it isn't.

MAN: Jason, get down! Everyone's looking at you! Please sit quietly.

JASON: But I want to look out of the window.

MAN: Come and sit with me.

JASON: But I want to sit here.

MAN: I'm sorry, but you must come and sit with me. And pick up that sweet paper. There are sweet papers everywhere. You know you mustn't drop litter on the floor.

JASON: It wasn't me. It was someone else.

MAN: Ssshh! Don't talk so loudly. *(to Diana)* I'm sorry about this.

DIANA: Don't worry. I know what it's like.

Answer:

What does Jason's father tell him to do?

What does he tell him he mustn't do?

Is Diana angry?

Set 1 Orders: direct and indirect

1.	INDIRECT	DIRECT
	Tell him/her to get down.	Get down!
	Tell him/her not to do that.	Don't do that!

Work in groups of three. One of you tells another to give orders to the third person in the group, who is a child. Look at the pictures. Start like this:

1. A: Tell her to wash her hands.
   B: Wash your hands!
   C: I don't want to!

2. A: Tell him not to sit so near the television.
   B: Don't sit so near the television!
   C: But I want to!

1. wash her hands

2. sit so near the television

3. be quiet

4. touch the fruit

5. hit the cat

6. brush her hair

2.

No smoking. You mustn't smoke.	Fasten seat belts. You must fasten your seat belts.

Look at the signs and notices. Put you must **or** you mustn't **in the following sentences. Complete the instructions where necessary.**

1. . . . . . walk across the road when the light is red.
2. . . . . . fasten your . . . . . when the sign is on.
3. . . . . . keep this entrance clear.
4. . . . . . drop . . . . . in the park or on the road.
5. . . . . . keep to the speed limit.
6. . . . . . take photographs in the theatre.
7. . . . . . go down this street because the sign says
   '. . . . .'
8. . . . . to other drivers.
9. . . . . . swim in the river.
10. . . . . . stop when you see the sign.
11. . . . . between 8.30 a.m. and 9.30 a.m.
12. . . . . . do a U turn in this main road.
13. . . . . . bring sandwiches into the classroom.
14. . . . . the animals.
15. . . . . . keep . . . . .

3. Many tourists do not understand the rules of a country that they are visiting. Make signs or notices for English-speaking visitors to your country for two of the following:

a popular beach   a public building
a beautiful tourist spot   a highway

Dialogue: Part 2

MAN: It's his half-term holiday. We went to Cambridge for the day.

JASON: I want some more chocolate.

DIANA: Did you have a nice time, Jason?

JASON: No, I didn't.

MAN: We went on the river and Jason got wet.

DIANA: Oh dear! Did you see King's College Chapel? It's very beautiful.

MAN: Yes, we did, but Jason didn't enjoy it very much.

JASON: No, I didn't. It was boring. And I lost my Startrek badge.

DIANA: Never mind, Jason. It's school again next week.

MAN: *(to Jason)* Here, have some more chocolate.

Answer:
Did Jason enjoy the river trip? Why not?
Did he enjoy seeing King's College Chapel?

Set 2   Past activities

1.	Did you have a nice weekend?	Yes, I did. It was lovely. It wasn't too bad. It was all right.

In pairs, ask and answer about the following:
weekend   holiday   evening   birthday   summer   Christmas

2.	What did you do?/Where did you go last summer?

In pairs, practise the conversation:
A: What did you do last summer?
B: We went to Torremolinos in Spain.
A: Did you have a good time?
B: Yes, we did. It was great!
A: Where did you stay?
B: In a small, family hotel.
A: Did you do anything special?
B: Yes, we went to a barbecue in the mountains. It was really good!

In pairs, roleplay similar conversations.

	Kirstin	John	Felicity	Frederick	Lesley
What did you do/ Where did you go	last summer?	last winter?	last winter?	last summer?	last winter?
	went scuba diving in Hawaii.	went hang gliding in the Dolomites in Italy.	went skiing in the mountains in Colorado.	went wind surfing in the Greek Islands.	went to the World Gymnastics Championships in Rumania.
Did you have a nice time?	Yes. Lovely!	Yes. Very good!	Yes. Great!	Yes. Marvellous!	Yes. Very interesting.
Where did you stay?	with friends	with my relatives	in a condominium	in a villa	in a hotel
Did you do anything special?	went on a boat trip and saw some whales.	went to Rome for a few days.	went to a night club in Aspen.	went to Delos and saw the ruins.	went to see Dracula's castle.

3. A classmate wrote about Kirstin in the college magazine, like this:

> Kirstin Brown had a lovely time last summer. She went scuba diving in Hawaii. She stayed with friends. She also went on a boat trip and saw some whales.

Write a few sentences about John and Felicity.

4. In pairs, talk about the weekend, your last summer holiday or your last winter holiday. Then write three or four sentences.

📼 Dialogue: Part 3

DIANA: Oh no! It's raining!

MAN: My car's in the station car park. Would you like a lift?

DIANA: It's all right. I can go by underground. It's only a short journey. My hotel's very near Tower Bridge Station.

MAN: That's on our way. We live in south-east London.

DIANA: Do you? Well, OK. Thank you. That's very kind of you. Goodness, this rain!

MAN: Would you like to borrow my umbrella? I don't mind the rain.

DIANA: Oh! Thanks.

MAN: Come on, Jason. Run and find our car.

Answer:
What's the weather like?
Where does the man live
How does he offer to help Diana?

Set 3 Offers of help

> **1.**   Would you like a lift?
> Would you like to borrow my umbrella?

In pairs, match the situations with the offers of help, like this:

A: I haven't got a notebook.
B: Would you like some paper?

SITUATION	OFFER
I haven't got a notebook.	to borrow my umbrella
I must catch the 9.30 plane.	to borrow a sweater
I haven't got any money.	some help with it
This exercise is difficult.	a lift to the airport
It's very cold in here.	some paper
It's raining.	to borrow my dictionary
I don't understand this word.	to borrow £5

2.   It's raining.
        Would you like to borrow my umbrella?
        Oh, thank you. That's very kind of you.

In pairs, use the situations in Exercise 1 to offer and accept help in the same way.

3.   It's raining.
        Would you like a lift?
        It's all right. I can go by underground.
        OK.

You are leaving school or work at the end of the day.
Offer a friend a lift in your car. In pairs, take turns to offer and refuse a lift. Choose from the following reasons each time:

—you are going to the cinema   —you are meeting a friend
—your sister is meeting you   —you have a car/bicycle
—you can walk   —you can catch a bus

Roleplay
Use the cues below to roleplay a telephone conversation with a friend. One of you was ill and didn't go to class yesterday.

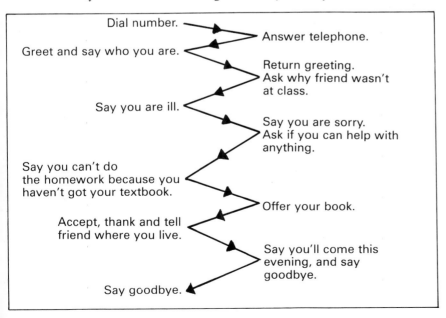

Dial number.
Answer telephone.
Greet and say who you are.
Return greeting. Ask why friend wasn't at class.
Say you are ill.
Say you are sorry. Ask if you can help with anything.
Say you can't do the homework because you haven't got your textbook.
Offer your book.
Accept, thank and tell friend where you live.
Say you'll come this evening, and say goodbye.
Say goodbye.

Reading

BREAK THE ICE

A GAME TO 'BREAK THE ICE' AT A PARTY

Divide your guests into pairs and count the number of pairs.

You must have the names of famous couples, e.g. Romeo and Juliet, Anthony and Cleopatra, Laurel and Hardy, Tarzan and Jane, Bonnie and Clyde.

Write each name clearly on a piece of paper. Pin one name on each person's back. They mustn't know who they are. Then tell each person to go round the room and ask questions. All the questions must have a 'yes/no' answer e.g. Am I American? Did I live in Hollywood? Was I in a book/film/children's story? etc.

They must find out who they are and find their partner. The first person to find his or her partner wins.

Answer:
How do you divide the guests?
What sort of names must you choose?
What do you do with each name?
Does each person know the name on his/her back?
What sort of questions must the guests ask?

Writing
Think of a party game you like to play in your country.
In pairs, write the instructions for the game.

🔘 Listening
Listen to Meg talking to a friend about her recent holiday in the States.
Note down the information to complete the chart:

Places visited:	
Where she stayed:	
Special occasion:	
Things that went wrong:	
Length of holiday:	
Her opinion of the holiday:	

Oral exercises

1. Respond to orders

A parent is telling his child what to do. Get down!
I don't want to get down!

1. Get down!
2. Sit still!
3. Eat your cornflakes!
4. Wash your hands!
5. Talk quietly!
6. Brush your hair!

2. Explain orders

A teacher is taking some children round a museum.
That sign says, 'Please don't touch the models.'
What does that mean, Jason?
That means we mustn't touch the models.
Good boy! Now that sign says, 'Please don't talk
loudly.' What does that mean, Jason?
That means we mustn't talk loudly.

1. Please don't touch the models.
2. Please don't talk loudly.
3. Please don't drop litter.
4. Please don't run.
5. No eating or drinking.
6. No smoking.

3. Give orders

You are looking after a small child.
CHILD: I don't want to brush my hair.
YOU: *But you must brush your hair.*
CHILD: I want to play in the street.
YOU: *But you mustn't play in the street.*

1. brush hair
2. play in the street
3. go to bed
4. play with the telephone
5. go to school
6. wash my hands

4. Ask about past events (1)

Ask Jason if he had a nice half-term.
Did you have a nice half-term, Jason?
No, I didn't. It was boring.

1. Ask Jason/a nice half-term.
2. Ask Diana/a good day in Cambridge.
3. Ask Joanne/a good day at the shops.
4. Ask Vince/a nice weekend.
5. Ask Paul/a nice evening at the theatre.
6. Ask Liz/a nice holiday in Scotland.

5. Ask about past events (2)

Ask Vince about his last trip to South America.
Ask where he stayed in Rio.
Where did you stay in Rio?

1. Ask where/stay/Rio.
2. Ask what/see/Rio.
3. Ask where/stay/Brasilia.
4. Ask how long/stay/São Paulo.
5. Ask how/travel/to Manaos.
6. Ask who/see/Salvador.

6. Answer about past events

A girl is talking to her friend about her holiday.
Did you go to Greece?
No, we didn't go to Greece. We went to Italy.

1. Go/Greece/Italy
2. Stay/a week/2 weeks
3. Stay/villa/hotel
4. Go to the seaside/sightseeing
5. Go/Florence/Rome
6. See/Coliseum/Vatican

Grammar

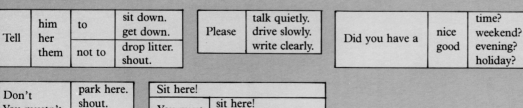

| Tell | him her them | to not to | sit down. get down. drop litter. shout. | | Please | talk quietly. drive slowly. write clearly. | | Did you have a | nice good | time? weekend? evening? holiday? |

| Don't You mustn't | park here. shout. touch. | | Sit here! | | | You must | sit here! park in the car park. |

| Would you like | a lift? to borrow my umbrella? | | It's all right. I can | catch a bus. go by underground. |

| What Where | did you | do? go? stay? | | I We | went | skiing. to Rome. stayed with relatives. |

🔊 **Dialogue: Part 1**

DIANA: Room 201, please.

WOMAN: Ah, Mrs Trent. The police want to see you.

DIANA: What's the matter? Is anything wrong?

WOMAN: This is Detective Inspector Platt from New Scotland Yard.

PLATT: How do you do, Mrs Trent. I'd like to ask you a few questions. Where did you go today?

DIANA: I went to Cambridge. I spent the day there.

PLATT: And when did you leave the hotel this morning?

DIANA: I left quite early. About eight o'clock.

PLATT: Who did you see before you left?

DIANA: I didn't see anyone!

Set 1   Past time

1.	Where did you go?	I went to Cambridge.
	When did you leave?	I left at eight o'clock.
	Who did you see?	I didn't see anyone.

Complete this questionnaire on what you did yesterday:

TIME	When did you get up?	I got up at . . .
	have breakfast?	I had breakfast . . .
	leave home?	I left home . . .
	start class/work?	I started class/ work . . .
	have lunch?	I had lunch . . .
	finish class/school/work?	I finished class/ school/work . . .
	get home?	I got home . . .
	have supper?	I had supper . . .
	go to bed?	I went to bed . . .
PEOPLE	Who did you talk to between 7 and 9?	I talked to . . .
	see before lunch?	I saw . . .
	have lunch with?	I had . . .
	sit next to in class?	I sat next to . . .
JOURNEY	How did you travel from home to school/work?	I came by. . .
		I walked to . . .
	How long did the journey take?	It took . . .
PLACE	Where did you have lunch?	I had . . .
	have coffee?	I had . . .
	have supper?	I had . . .
	do your homework?	I did . . .
CLOTHES	What clothes did you wear?	I wore . . .
FREE TIME	What about other activities?	I played . . .
	What else did you do?	I visited . . .
		I watched . . .
		I went . . .
		I saw. . .
		I bought . . .

2. In pairs, ask your partner what he/she did yesterday. Ask the questions from the questionnaire.

3. Some people broke into your school last Sunday. The police think that they broke in sometime between 8 a.m. and 4 p.m. The police question everyone in your class. Write sentences to say exactly what you did between 8 and 4 last Sunday.

Answer:
What time did Diana leave the hotel?
Where was Diana all day?
Who is Platt?
What three questions did he ask Diana?

🔊 Dialogue: Part 2

DIANA: I'm sorry, but what is all this about? Why are you asking me these questions?

PLATT: I'm afraid someone broke into your room today.

DIANA: Oh no! What did they take? Not my film, I hope. I'm showing it tomorrow.

PLATT: I don't know, Mrs Trent.

DIANA: But why did they break in? I can't understand it.

PLATT: Did you go to Cambridge alone?

DIANA: Yes, I did. My colleague, Mr Roberts, was here at the conference.

PLATT: Oh, was he?

DIANA: Yes, he was.

PLATT: Doesn't your colleague go into your room sometimes?

DIANA: No, Inspector, he doesn't. No one goes into my room.

PLATT: Let's go and have a look. Let's find out if there's anything missing.

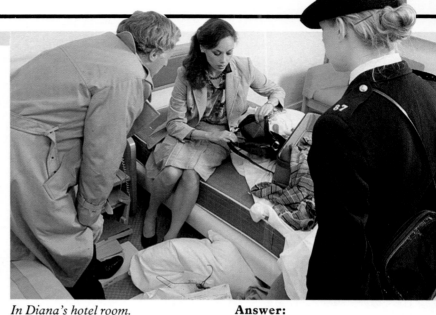

In Diana's hotel room.

DIANA: Oh no! The film! It's not here.

PLATT: Is anything else missing?

DIANA: No, just the film.

PLATT: But why. Mrs Trent? Why does someone want your film?

Answer:

Why are the police at the hotel?

Why is Diana worried about her film?

When the Inspector asks, 'Doesn't your colleague go into your room sometimes?', does he expect the answer 'yes' or 'no'?

What is missing from Diana's room?

Set 2 Surprise and interest

1.	My colleague was here at the conference. Oh, was he?

Practise these short conversations:

GIVE INFORMATION →	EXPRESS SURPRISE → AND INTEREST	SAY SOMETHING ELSE
A	B	A
I'm English. →	Oh, are you? →	Yes, I come from Brighton.
She's a teacher.	Oh, is she?	Yes, she teaches English.
I come from Greece.	Oh, do you?	Yes, I go back there every summer.
I don't like tea.	Oh, don't you?	No, I always drink coffee.
She speaks English.	Oh, does she?	Yes, she speaks it very well.
He doesn't work.	Oh, doesn't he?	No, he's unemployed.
He was ill.	Oh, was he?	Yes, he stayed in bed all day.
He wasn't at school.	Oh, wasn't he?	No, he was ill.
She went to London.	Oh, did she?	Yes, she stayed at the Tower Hotel.
She didn't enjoy it.	Oh, didn't she?	No, she lost her money.

2. In pairs, have conversations about the people at the conference. Express surprise and interest, and say something else about them. Use the information on the right, like this:

A: Diana Trent is a film director.
B: Oh, is she?
A: Yes, she works for Focus Film and Video.
B: Oh, does she?
A: Yes, and she's married.
B: Oh, is she?
A: Yes, and she has a daughter.
B: Oh, has she?
A: Yes, and she went to Bristol University.
B: Oh, did she?

3. In pairs, say something about yourselves. Comment with surprise and interest, and add more information, as in Exercise 2. Choose from the following topics:

	Begin like this:
Sports and games you like and take part in.	I like playing . . .
A recent holiday and special things you did.	Last year I went to . . .
Favourite TV programmes and TV stars.	My favourite programme(s) is/are . . .
Free time activities and where you do them.	I like/play. . .
Interesting details about your relations, family or friends.	My sister works . . . My neighbour. . .
Something you know about a national figure.	(name) lives/is married to/owns . . .

Set 3 Confirmation

Isn't Diana Trent a film director?
That's right, she is.
And doesn't she work for Focus Film and Video?
Yes, she does.
Didn't she go to Bristol University?
That's right, she did.

In pairs, ask and answer about Paul, Vince and Joanne in the same way. Make negative questions each time to show that you expect your partner to agree with you.

DIANA TRENT,
film director for Focus Film and Video. Married with one daughter. Went to Bristol University

PAUL ROBERTS
cameraman for Focus Film and Video. Went to Wolverhampton Technical College

VINCE HALL
sound technician for the Sight and Sound Company. Married with three children Went to night school in Detroit

JOANNE TESSLER
film assistant for Sight and Sound Company. Comes from California lives in Los Angeles. Went to University of Southern California

🔊 Dialogue: Part 3

INSPECTOR: Mrs Trent, can you answer a few more questions, please? I want you to tell me about Mr Roberts . . .

DIANA: Paul? He's my colleague, Inspector. He and I made the film. He didn't steal it.

INSPECTOR: Perhaps not. But can you ask him to come and see me, please?

DIANA: All right.

INSPECTOR: Oh, just one moment, Mrs Trent. Who else knew you were in Cambridge?

DIANA: No one knew. Oh, wait a moment! I think Vince and Joanne, some American friends, knew.

INSPECTOR: I see. Well, I want to see them, too. Can you ask them not to leave the hotel?

DIANA: Yes, of course. But why?

INSPECTOR: You want to get your film back, don't you Mrs Trent?

DIANA: Yes, I do, Inspector. I certainly do.

Answer:
What does the Inspector want Diana to do? List four things.
Why does the Inspector want to see Paul and the Americans?

Set 4   Requests

> 1.   Can you answer a few questions, please?

Look at the pictures and make requests. Answer with Yes, of course **each time.**

> 2.   Can you ask him to come and see me, please?

close the window

answer the telephone

open the door

post this letter

In pairs, read this conversation when Paul meets Diana in the hotel foyer:

DIANA: Oh, Paul. Can you do me a favour?

PAUL: Yes, certainly.

DIANA: Can you ask Vince and Joanne to come and see me this morning?

PAUL: Yes, of course.

Use the information in the chart to roleplay similar conversations:

WHO MEETS WHO?	WHO'S THE MESSAGE FOR?	WHAT'S THE MESSAGE?
Vince/Paul	Joanne	Meet me in the coffee bar after lunch.
Receptionist/Japanese tour leader	The Japanese group	Leave their luggage in the foyer this morning.
Receptionist/American tour leader	The CBS group	Meet me in the foyer after breakfast.

3.	I want you to tell me about Mr Roberts. Can you ask them not to leave the hotel?

Read the note on the right which Liz wrote to Doug:

Answer:
What does Liz want the milkman to do?
(She wants him to leave . . .)
What doesn't she want him to do?
(She doesn't want him to leave anything . . .)
What does she want the builders to do?
What does she want the video hire man to do?
What doesn't she want the gardener to do?

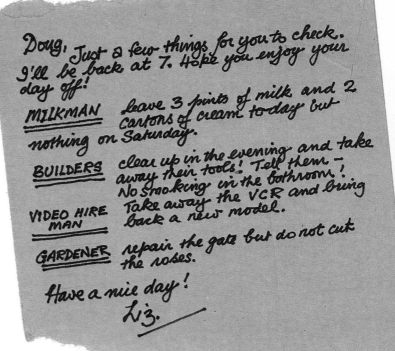

Doug,
Just a few things for you to check.
I'll be back at 7. Hope you enjoy your day off!

MILKMAN leave 3 pints of milk and 2 cartons of cream today but nothing on Saturday.

BUILDERS clear up in the evening and take away their tools! Tell them — No smoking in the bathroom!

VIDEO HIRE MAN Take away the VCR and bring back a new model.

GARDENER repair the gate but do not cut the roses.

Have a nice day!
Liz.

Write the note again, but this time write the instructions out in full. Use:

Can you ask	him her them	to . . .? not to . . .?

Start like this:
Can you ask the milkman to leave . . ., but ask him not to leave anything on . . .?
Can you ask the builders to . . ., and ask them not to . . .?

⊙⊙ Open dialogue
Talk to Liz.

LIZ: Oh hello. Don't I know you? Aren't you from Lyon in France?
YOU: . . . .
LIZ: Oh, are you? Sorry! Tell me, when do your classes finish this term?
YOU: . . . .
LIZ: Oh, do they?
YOU: . . . .
LIZ: Well, aren't you pleased with your English now?
YOU: . . . .
LIZ: Do you know anyone English?
YOU: . . . .
LIZ: Keep working hard! Bye for now!
YOU: . . . .

Roleplay
Work in threes. One of you is a parent, the other two are teenagers. It is after midnight. Your son/daughter (aged 14) went out at 7.30 p.m. and said he/she was going to a friend's house. He/She is still not back. You are very angry. Suddenly your son/daughter returns. Ask and find out exactly what he/she did between 7.30 and midnight. Then telephone the friend and ask him/her the same questions. See if the answers are the same! Ask questions like these:
What time did you meet?   Where did you meet/go?   How did you get there?

🔲 Listening

Some burglars broke into the sports pavilion of a local school. They broke several windows and stole some silver cups and statues. Listen to Police Constable Mackenzie questioning two young people.

How many questions does he ask them about time? (When?/What time?)
about people? (Who?)
about places? (Where?)

Reading

Win, 42, tells how she met her husband:

I remember I was about 19. I went to a dance at the village hall. I went with my best friend, Marjorie. Marjorie was very pretty and all the boys liked her. They all wanted to dance with her. I didn't enjoy dances much. I was always very shy.

I sat at a table in the corner of the dance hall. No one asked me to dance. After about an hour, Marjorie came up to me and said, 'Go and ask one of the boys to dance! You can't just sit there!'

It was awful. I hated every minute of it. In the end she told one of her boyfriends to go and ask me for a dance. I was so embarrassed! Anyway, the boy came up and we danced. His name was Mick and he was very nice. He asked me to go to the cinema with him the next day. That was the start of it. I went out with him for a year, and then he asked me to marry him. My parents were a bit surprised. They liked him, but they said we were too young. They told us to wait. We waited nine months and then, on my 21st birthday, we got married. We now have three children and we're very happy. I still see Marjorie quite often. She always says, 'You mustn't sit and wait for things to happen. You must go out and make them happen.' I think she's right!

Answer:

Where did Win meet her husband, Mick?
How old was she then?
Who was she with?
What was her friend like?
Why didn't Win enjoy dances?
Why wasn't she happy at first at this dance?
What did Marjorie tell her to do? Did Win do it?
What did Marjorie do then?
Who came up and asked Win to dance?
Did he ask to see her again?
What happened after a year?
Why didn't Win's parents want them to get married?
When did they get married?
Are they happy now?
What does Marjorie always say?

Writing

Look at the reading text on page 58 and answer these questions with short notes.
When did they get up?
What did they do after breakfast?
Where did they go after lunch?
What did they do all day in the park?
When did they leave the park?
What did they do at home?

Then write a paragraph describing how the family spent Sunday.

Oral exercises

1. Ask for and give past details (1) (Open exercise)
When did you get up today?
I got up at 6 o'clock.

1. When/get up/today?
2. When/arrive here?
3. Who/see first/today?
4. What/have for breakfast/this morning?
5. How much/spend on food/yesterday?

2. Ask for and give past details (2) (Open exercise)
Where did you go last weekend?
I went to see my grandparents.
I didn't go anywhere.
I stayed at home.

Talk about:
1. last weekend   3. last Easter
2. last Christmas   4. last summer

3. Express surprise and interest
Some burglars broke into the school.
Did they?
Yes, they did.

1. It was at the weekend.
2. They stole the book money.
3. It was about £500.
4. I know one of them.
5. He's my neighbour.

4. Ask people to give instructions
You are a member of the cabin crew of
BA Flight 307.
Read the list of instructions, and tell a new colleague
what to do.

They must fasten their seatbelts
Can you ask them to fasten their seatbelts.
They mustn't smoke.
Can you ask them not to smoke.

1. They must fasten their seatbelts.
2. They mustn't smoke.
3. They must put their seats upright.
4. They must finish their drinks.
5. They mustn't stand in the gangway.

5. Ask people to make requests
You are a teacher in charge of a class of students
going on an outing. Your assistant teacher wants some
information.

Where do you want the students to meet?
Ask them to meet at the railway station.

1. Where to meet?/railway station
2. When to meet?/4 p.m.
3. What food to bring?/some fruit for the journey
4. How much money to bring?/about £5
5. What clothes to wear?/a warm jacket, a sweater
   and some jeans

Grammar

Regular past tenses

finish	finished
like	liked
play	played
rain	rained
start	started
walk	walked

Irregular past tenses

have	had	do	did	lose	lost
get	got	pay	paid	steal	stole
leave	left	wear	wore	tell	told
go	went	see	saw	meet	met
sit	sat	come	came	drive	drove
take	took	break	broke	say	said

Where		go?
Who	did you	see?
When		leave?

I didn't	see anyone.(?)
Did you	

Someone	broke into your room.
No one	

I	don't	want	you	to	go to	the party.
She	doesn't		him		leave	
			them			

Ask	him	to	come and see me.
	her	not to	arrive late.

He	asked	me	to	dance.
	told		not to	speak.

Aren't you	English?
Isn't he	
Weren't you	ill?
Wasn't he	
Don't you	live in Leeds?
Doesn't he	
Didn't you go to Bristol?	
Isn't there a bar?	

I'm	English.
He's	
I	was ill.
He	
I live	in Leeds.
He lives	
I went to Bristol.	
There's a bar.	

Oh, are you?
Oh, is he?
Oh, were you?
Oh, was he?
Oh, do you?
Oh, does he?
Oh, did you?
Oh, is there?

Can you	answer some questions?
	post this letter?

🔊 Dialogue: Part 1

JOANNE: So you got your film back?

PAUL: Yes, luckily. They caught a man at the airport.

JOANNE: What?

PAUL: Yes, I'll tell you about it later. Shall we go in now?

JOANNE: Whose film is showing?

PAUL: The Italians'. Ours is on after theirs. I think we're going to win.

JOANNE: Well, it's certainly a topical subject.

PAUL: Yes, and it's political. A lot of important people aren't going to like it . . .

Answer:
What's the title of the film?
What's it about?
What time does it start?
Whose film is showing before this?
Whose film does Paul think is going to win?
Who do you think the 'important people' are?
Why aren't they going to like the film?

iNTERVID
International Video Conference
Documentary Section
INVITATION
You are invited to the British première of a new film from Focus Film and Video
"**So you think you're safe?**"
—the true facts about nuclear power in Europe!
Tuesday May 18th at 11·30 a.m.
Cinema A

Set 1 Predictions

1.	I think we're going to win a prize.
	People aren't going to like it.

I	am			
You	are	(not)		
He/she	is		going to	win.
We	are	(n't)		like it.
They	are			

Am	I		
Are	you	going to	win?
Is	she/he		like it?
Are	we		
	they		

Say what is, or isn't, going to happen in the pictures below. Choose the right verb from the list.

score a goal   jump the fence   eat her food   cry   get married   catch the ball

2. You are going to visit an astrologer to find out about your future. Write down the questions you want to ask. Ask about:

ROMANTIC LIFE   MONEY   HOME LIFE   WORK   EDUCATION   TRAVEL

Start like this:

Am I going to | get a good job?
              | change my job?

Set 2 Identification

1.	Whose is this pen?	It's mine.
	Is this your book?	No, it's Maria's
	Whose are these gloves?	They're hers/his.
	Whose are these books?	They're ours/yours/theirs

Collect a few personal belongings such as exercise books, pens, bags, textbooks, dictionaries etc. Put them together on a desk and, in turns, find out who they belong to by asking questions like those in the box above.

| 2. | Whose is the Cadillac? It's the Conways'. |
| | Whose is the Volkswagen? It's mine. |

You are a member of a Custom Car Club. In pairs, choose either the Volkswagen or the Volvo. Use the chart to find the owners of each car.

MAKE OF CAR	COLOUR	OWNER
Volkswagen	Green	Student 1
Volvo	Red	Student 2
Ford	Silver and Gold	Anita and Paul Wilson
Cadillac	Blue and red	Jack and Kim Conway
Pinto	Red	Philip Webb
Mustang	Black	Jessica Gregg

In pairs, describe each car, like this:

> Which is the Conways' car? Theirs is the blue and red one with stars and stripes on it.
> Which is your car? Mine is the green one with yellow flowers on it.

Write sentences describing each car, like this:

> The Conways' car is a blue and red Cadillac with stars and stripes on it.

3.	running shoes	do you like?	I like the red ones.
Which	ones		I quite like the ones with stripes on them.
	sports bag		I like the green one.
	one		I quite like the one with the Tiger label on it.

In pairs, talk about the following sports clothes and equipment in the same way:

running shoes   sports bags   T-shirts   shorts   rollerskates

🎧 Dialogue: Part 2

DIANA: Isn't it marvellous? We won.

VINCE: Congratulations! The film was really great.

DIANA: Yes, I'm really pleased. We've worked on it for over two years. Let's order some champagne. And what about something to eat?

Have you had lunch yet?

VINCE: No, we haven't. That sounds a good idea.

(later)

WAITER: You look happy!

DIANA: Yes, we won a Silver Star award. Can you pour the champagne, please?

WAITER: With pleasure.

Answer:

What time of day is it?

Why is Diana happy?

Did Vince like the film?

What are they going to drink?

Set 3 Recent activities

1.	Have you had lunch yet?
	Yes, I have./No, I haven't.
	I've had/haven't had lunch.

🔖 Dialogue: Part 3

Complete the questionnaire below, and then ask and answer about each activity, like this:

Have you had breakfast today? Yes, I have./No, I haven't.

		YES/NO
MEALS	Have you had breakfast today? lunch yet? supper yet?	
REFRESHMENTS	Have you had a cup of coffee today? a cup of tea yet? a soft drink yet?	
JOBS IN THE HOME	Have you made your bed today? tidied your room? washed up the breakfast things?	
OTHER ACTIVITIES	Have you read a newspaper today? had a shower today? done your homework? bought anything today? played tennis/football this week?	

2. Talk about your partner's recent activities, like this:

(Name of partner) has had breakfast today, but he/she hasn't had lunch yet.

Talk about four or five activities.

3. Write five sentences about your own activities, like this:

I've had breakfast today, but I haven't had supper yet.

4.	How long have you worked on the film?
	We've worked on it for over two years.

Ask and answer these questions in pairs:

How long have you lived in this town/city/in your present home?
How long have you been in this school/college/class/room?

Write five sentences about your partner, like this:

1. Juan has lived in Mexico City for sixteen years.
2. He has . . .

WOMAN: Mrs Trent, your taxi is here.
DIANA: Oh, thank you.
WOMAN: Which suitcase is yours?
DIANA: Mine's the brown one with the white straps. Well, everyone, I'm afraid it's time to go.

VINCE: Goodbye, Diana, and good luck. It was great meeting you.

DIANA: Goodbye, Vince. Goodbye, Joanne. Take care of yourselves. 'Bye Paul. See you in Manchester.

WOMAN: Excuse me. Whose is this silver star?

DIANA: Oh sorry! It's mine. It's our award! Goodbye, everyone!

Answer:
Why has the taxi arrived at the hotel?
What does Diana's suitcase look like?
Whose is the silver star?
What is it?
What do you think Vince is going to do now?
What about Paul and Joanne?

Reading

Sylvana Scarlatti answers an advertisement for a summer job in Wales.
Here is her letter:

HOLIDAY JOBS ✳

Camp Australia, Camp America—
now Camp Wales!

Over 18's, students, teachers, social
workers. Holiday work with Camp
Wales - Free flights, free board, work
permit and pocket money. Spend nine
weeks (July~August) in a Welsh
Summer Camp teaching sports, arts
and crafts. The camp is in the
beautiful mountains of North Wales.
Two free weeks for travel around
Britain. Details from Camp Wales.
146 Queen Anne's Avenue,
London, SW7 4HR.

```
                                        c/o Mrs Bennett
                                        33, Queen Anne Gardens,
                                        London.    SE5  6HR


        Camp Organiser
        Summer Camp Limited,
        Camp Wales,
        146 Queen Anne's Avenue,
        London       SW7  4HR



        Dear Sir,

        My name is Sylvana Scarlatti and I am 21 years old.  I am
        Italian and I am from Milan.

        I have studied English for five years and I am taking the
        Cambridge First Certificate examination in June this year.
        I am studying English at the moment at the Tower School of
        English in London.  I have been here for four months.  I also
        speak French and a little German.

        I have had some experience with children before.  Last
        summer I went to Boston and looked after three young children.

        I like swimming, walking and all outdoor sports.  I would like
        to work at Camp Wales very much.  I am going to be an interpreter
        so I want to speak good English.

        You can contact me either c/o Mrs Bennett at the above address,
        or c/o The Tower Language School, River Road, London E2  2RF.
        I am free from July 1st.

        I am looking forward to hearing from you,

        Sylvana Scarlatti
        Sylvana Scarlatti
```

**The camp organiser sends Sylvana an application form for the job.
Copy and fill it in for her.**

Camp Wales, 146 Queen Anne's Avenue, London SW7 4HR

Summer Camp Limited

Application for SUMMER CAMP LEADERS
WRITE CLEARLY   USE BLOCK CAPITALS

NAME _____
ADDRESS _____

NATIONALITY _____
AGE _____
EXAMINATIONS _____
(please state any examinations you are preparing for) _____
Are you a native speaker of English? _____ If not state length of study of English _____
RELEVANT EXPERIENCE _____ INTERESTS _____
Address for Correspondence _____ First date you can start work _____

Writing

1. Make and fill in a form for yourself to apply for a job at Camp Wales.
2. Write a letter like Sylvana's applying for a job.

Oral exercises

1. Predict the weather
What's the weather like today?
I think it's going to be fine.

1. fine
2. wet
3. hot
4. cold
5. warm
6. to rain

2. Talk about future events
Any news of your parents?
Yes. They're going to move to the south coast.
Oh, really?

1. your parents/move to the south coast
2. Diana/make a film in America
3. your brother/change his job
4. Mary and Simon/get married
5. Paul/work in Los Angeles for a year
6. your sister/have a baby

3. Talk about uncompleted activities
Are you coming with me?
No. I haven't had breakfast yet.

1. have breakfast
2. get dressed
3. have a shower
4. make the beds
5. tidy the house

4. Talk about completed activities
Have you done your homework this morning?
Yes. I did it before breakfast.

1. do your homework
2. do your exercises
3. make your bed
4. read the new lesson
5. tidy your bedroom
6. write the exercises

5. Identify belongings
Which is your hat?
This is mine.
Which is Paul's bag?
This is his.

1. your hat
2. Paul's bag
3. our tickets
4. my umbrella
5. Liz's bike
6. the Conways' house

6. Describe clothes
Which dress do you like?
I like the white one with the silver stripes on it.

1. dress/white/silver stripes
2. shorts/green/Ellesse label
3. running shoes/white/black stripes
4. sports bag/red/picture of Snoopy
5. sweatshirt/blue/big star

Grammar

Possessive adjectives	Possessive pronouns
my	mine
your	yours
his	his
her	hers
its	its
our	ours
their	theirs

Whose		
	is	this car?
	are	these gloves?
	car	is this?
	gloves	are these?

This is	my car.
	Jack's car.
	the Conways' car.

Which	T-shirt(s) one(s)	do you like?
I like the	red one(s) one(s)	with the star	on	it. them.

Have	you they	had lunch yet?
Has	he she	

I You We They	've haven't	had lunch (yet).
He She	has hasn't	

I	am	not going to going to	win a prize.
You	are		
He/she	is		
We	are		
They	are		

How long	have	you they	been lived	here?
	has	he she		

For three weeks.

Famous lives
a game for two players

What you need
You each need two pieces of paper and a dice.
Draw two charts like those below.
The aim of the game is to complete
the charts for two famous
people chosen from
pages 118 and 119.

1. NAME OF PERSON — Louis Braille
2. NATIONALITY
3. DATE OF BIRTH AND DEATH
4. PROFESSION — Teacher.
5. REASON FOR FAME
6. INTERESTING FACTS ABOUT HIS/HER LIFE

How to play
Take it in turns with your partner to throw the dice. The first
person to throw a 1 starts. If this is you, ask your partner to
choose a name for you. Write in the name next to number 1 on
your first chart. Pass the dice to your partner.

When it is your turn again, throw the dice and see what number
you get. If it is, for example, a 4, you must ask your partner the
profession of your famous person. For example, 'What did Louis
Braille do?' Your partner must look at the paragraph about
Louis Braille, find the answer and say, 'He was a teacher.' You
write in the answer next to number 4 on the chart.

If you get a 1 the next time you throw the dice, you can start
your second chart. If you throw a 6, you can have another turn.
The first person to complete all the sections for both the famous
people has won.

Useful expressions
Whose turn is it?
It's mine/yours.
It's my/your turn now.
What does . . . mean?
I need a 3/4.
Oh dear, I've got that.
Good, I haven't got that.
Is that/That isn't the right answer(?).
I/You won!

Questions
1. Which person are you going to choose for me?
2. What nationality was he/she?
3. When was he/she born and when did he/she die?
4. What did he/she do?
5. What was he/she famous for?
6. Can you tell me something interesting about his/her life?

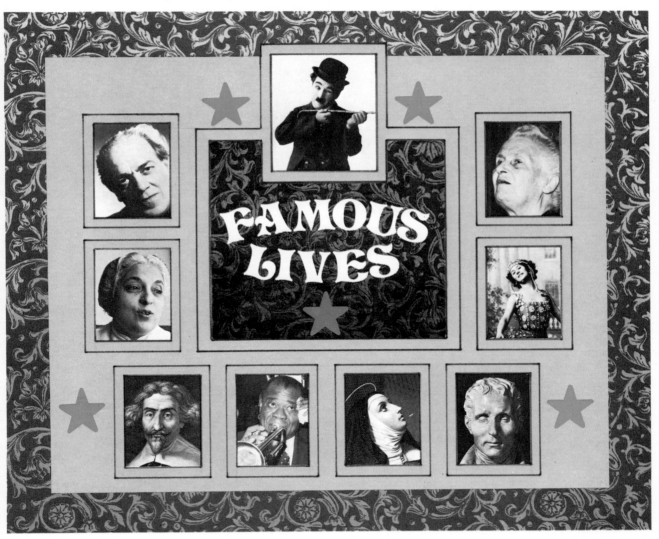

Louis Armstrong
American (1900-71)

Louis Armstrong was a trumpeter, a bandleader and a singer. For half his life he was billed as 'The World's Greatest Trumpeter.' His influence on jazz was greater than any other musician. The man they called 'Satchmo' spent his early life in New Orleans, and as a child sang in the streets for money. Some of his most famous songs were 'Hello Dolly', 'Mack the Knife', and 'When the Saints Go Marching In'.

Nelly Bly
American (1865-1922)

Her real name was Elizabeth Cochrane Seaman, but she changed it to Nelly Bly after a famous song. She was one of the most adventurous journalists in America in the last century. In 1890 she went round the world by boat, train and horse. It took just over 72 days, faster than in Jules Verne's novel *Around the World in 80 Days*. Apart from travelling, she fought actively for social, economic and sexual equality.

Louis Braille
French (1809-52)

Louis Braille became blind at the age of three. As an adult he was a teacher at the Institute of Blind Youth in Paris. Here he invented a system of reading for blind people, called the Braille System. This consists of embossed dots on a page so that blind people can 'read' the letters by touch.

Miguel de Cervantes Saavedra
Spanish (1547-1616)

Cervantes was a writer and dramatist. He was nearly sixty when he wrote the famous *Don Quixote*. After the Bible, this is the most translated book in the world. The work of Cervantes influenced many later writers, including Dickens and the Russian writer, Dostoevsky.

Sir Charles Chaplin
English (1889-1977)

Sir Charles Chaplin, better known as Charlie Chaplin, has become the best-known comic actor in the history of the cinema. He went to America to live in 1914. There he invented his famous comic character for the cinema. It was a tramp — the little man who always won. He acted in many films, but the classics are *The Gold Rush, City Lights* and *Modern Times*.

Maria Montessori
Italian (1870-1952)

Maria Montessori was a teacher. She ran a special school for backward children in Rome. She helped these children to learn to read, write and count, by the age of six, or sometimes younger. Through her books, *The Montessori Method* and *The Advanced Montessori Method* (for older children) she has changed the teaching of young children all over the world.

Vijaya Lakshmi Pandit
Indian (1900-)

Vijaya Lakshmi Pandit was a politician. She became famous for being the first woman president of the United Nations. She came from the Nehru family. Her brother, Jawaharlal, and her brother's daughter, Indira, both became Prime Minister of India. She herself held many political posts including ambassador to Moscow, the United States, and Mexico. Besides this, she was a strong campaigner for racial equality.

Anna Pavlova
Russian (1885-1931)

Anna Pavlova is the most famous ballet dancer of all time. She started training at the Imperial Ballet School in St Petersburg (Leningrad) at the age of ten. Ten years later she became a prima ballerina. Most people remember her for her performance in *Swan Lake.* She has helped to make ballet popular on a world-wide scale.

Teresa of Avila
Spanish (1515-82)

St Teresa of Avila was a nun. At the age of eighteen, she joined the Carmelite order. Between 1568 and 1580 she founded seventeen convents and four monasteries. The Church was always against her, and she was often sick. In 1622 Pope Gregory XV made her a saint.

Heitor Villa-Lobos
Brazilian (1887-1959)

Villa-Lobos was the first Latin-American composer to win an international reputation. He wrote twelve symphonies, five piano concertos and a number of songs. He also wrote guitar music. Much of his music is in the style of Brazilian folk music. One of his most famous pieces of music, *Bachianas Brasileiras,* puts the music of Bach into a Brazilian style.

Vivien Leigh as Scarlett O'Hara
Clark Gable as Rhett Butler

Scarlett outside her home, Tara

David O. Selznick

At the Academy Awards ceremony for 1939,
Gone with the Wind won eight awards, including an award for
the best actress of the year and for the best direction.

The book

In 1926 Margaret Mitchell, a journalist and housewife from
Atlanta, Georgia, started to write a book. She finished it ten
years later. It was called *Gone with the Wind.* It became the most
popular American novel of all time.

It is a long, romantic and exciting novel. It is about a
beautiful young woman, Scarlett O'Hara and twelve years in her
life just before, during and after the American Civil War
(1862-64). In the book Scarlett marries Rhett Butler, the tall,
dark and handsome hero, but she doesn't love him. All the time
she loves someone else. But the man she loves is married.

The film

David O. Selznick, Hollywood film producer, decided to make a
film of *Gone with the Wind.* He chose a famous film star of the
time, Clark Gable, for the part of Rhett Butler, but he could not
find anyone for the part of Scarlett. He searched and searched
for two and a half years. No one was quite right. In the end,
there was no more time. Plans for the film were ready. On the
night of December 10th, 1938, all the cameras were ready to film
an important scene in the film – the burning of the city of
Atlanta. Selznick still did not have an actress for Scarlett.

At the time, Vivien Leigh, a young British actress, was in
Hollywood with her fiancé, Laurence Olivier. Selznick's brother,
Myron, knew the couple and asked them to come and watch the
fire scene. He took them to the studios, found his brother,
David, and tapped him on the shoulder. David O. Selznick
turned round. There, in the light of the fire, he saw the
beautiful face of Vivien Leigh. 'David, here's your Scarlett,'
Myron said. Vivien Leigh won the most famous part in the
history of the cinema – Scarlett O'Hara, the heroine of *Gone
with the Wind.*

The première

It was a long and difficult film to make, but on December 11th,
1939 Selznick sent this telegram to a colleague:
HAVE JUST FINISHED GONE WITH THE WIND. GOD
BLESS US ALL. SCREENING AT TWO TOMORROW
TUESDAY FOR 750 JOURNALISTS.

The film was nearly four hours long. At the end the journalists
sat quietly for a moment and then they cheered and cheered.

On the day of the première the Mayor of Atlanta closed all the
schools and public buildings. *Gone with the Wind* became a
famous film and it made a lot of money. They called it 'the
greatest motion picture of all time'.

Make questions for these answers. Use the question words suggested.

WHO?
1. the author of the book (*Example:* Who was Margaret Mitchell?)
2. the producer of *Gone with the Wind*
3. Rhett Butler, Scarlett's husband in the film

WHERE?
4. from Atlanta, Georgia
5. at the studios on the night of December 10th
6. from Britain

HOW LONG?
7. ten years
8. two and a half years
9. nearly four hours

WHEN?
10. in 1926
11. on December 10th 1938
12. on December 11th 1939

WHAT?
13. Laurence Olivier
14. It's about the life of a beautiful young woman called Scarlett O'Hara during the American Civil War.
15. They cheered and cheered.

WHY?
16. Because no one was quite right for the part.
17. Because David's brother, Myron, knew them and had asked them to come.
18. Because she loved another man.
19. Because the story was set in Atlanta, Georgia.
20. Because at that time people liked romantic and exciting novels.

I loved it. I first saw it in 1940 and I loved it then. They don't make films like that any more. John aged 60.

I didn't like it. It was too long and sentimental. The acting was bad, the music was too loud and the story was stupid. Linda aged 24.

I liked it very much. It was very exciting. Clark Gable was great and so was Vivien Leigh, but I didn't like the other man very much. Steve aged 16.

The greatest film in the world? Who said that? It was boring. I've seen much better films than that. Greg aged 32.

Discuss

Have you ever seen *Gone with the Wind?*
If so, when did you see it?
Did you enjoy it?
If not, would you like to see it?
What sort of films do you like?
Make a list of five films you have seen recently. Find out if anyone else in the class has seen them, and if they enjoyed them.

📼 Listening

Listen to two students, A and B, talking about their stay in Britain. Fill in the chart below with information about them as you listen.

	A	B
Name:		
Country of origin:		
Purpose of visit to Britain:		
Place of study:		
Length of study:		
Present address:		
Interests:		
Family:		
Length of time spent in Britain:		
Date of return home:		
Ambitions:		

Listen again and make a note of the questions the interviewer uses.
Now interview your partner, and make notes about him or her.
Write about your partner and yourself for homework.

Words and expressions to remember

Unit 1
address
hotel
key
name
number
receptionist
room
telephone

be (am, is, are)
phone
write

double

in

What?

and
or

Good morning.
Good afternoon.
Good evening.
Here's . . . .
No.
Oh good!
please
Thank you.
Thanks.
Yes.

Mr
Mrs
Miss
Ms

Numbers 1-10

Unit 2
book
class
comb

country
diary
dictionary
exercise
exercise book
flag
friend
identity card
map
nationality
pen
pencil
purse
school
student
taxi
teacher
ticket
umbrella
wallet

come
meet

big
good
new
nice
polite
small

here
(over) there
too
very

---

all
this
that

from

Where?

but

Excuse me!
Goodbye.
Hello.
Hi.
How do you do.
in English
Pleased to meet you.

America
American
Britain
British

Unit 3
animal(s)
baby (ies)
boy (s)
brother (s)
cat (s)
centre
child (ren)
classical
 music
coast
coffee
company
cup (s)
doctor (s)
dog (s)
film
first name
flat
girl (s)
house (s)
housewife (ves)
job
man (men)
people
place (s)
pop music
secretary (ies)
sister (s)
surname
town
woman (en)

do
go
have
like
live
make
mean
spell
study
teach
work

first
married
unemployed
young

called
out
very much
both

---

by
for
near
of
on
with

east
north
south
west

Fine, thanks.
How are you?
I don't know.
I don't understand.
Let's go out.
Not too bad, thanks.
OK.
Really?
Very well, thank you.
What does that mean?

England

Unit 4
biscuit
box
café
cake
cathedral
cheese
chocolate
cinema
concert
disco
drink
glass
home
language
letter
milk
orange
packet
party
pence
piece
pound
record
sandwich
sports
tea
television
theatre
water

can (ability)
can (request)
cook
drive
hate
love
play
read
ride
see
sightsee
sing
sit
smoke
speak
swim
type
walk
want
watch

---

black
late
old
white

about
a little
at all
at home
just (= only)
lots of
soon
years old

these
those

round
to

How much?
How old?
Who?

Dear . . . ,
It's great fun.
See you later.
Sorry!
That's all right.
There you are.

Nor do I.
So do I.

Numbers
 10-1,000,000

Unit 6
bank
bar
bus
camera
car
cassette
clock
conference
flight
flower
football
half
ice cream
match
meeting
money
morning
newspaper
night
parcel
plane
postcard
post office
programme
quarter
restaurant
shoe
shop
soap
stamp
stranger
street
toothpaste
tourist
train
video
week
wine

---

arrive
ask
book (v)
buy
close
finish
get
hurry
leave
must
open
rent
send
start
turn

busy
early
fun
interesting
last (night)
lovely
this (morning)

again
left
now
o'clock
quite
right
today
together
yesterday

some
many
most

after
at (+ place)
at (+ time)
before
in (+ parts of the day)
next to
opposite
past (with clock hours)
to (with clock hours)
until

How?
What time?
When?

Bye!
How funny!
See you soon!
Thank you very much.

Unit 7
beach
beer
bicycle
boat
bread
breakfast
butter
canteen
church
city
college
daughter
day
exercises
family
father
floor
fruit
hour

husband
lunch
mother
parent
park
photograph
pub
son
song
story
supper
table
weather
wife

catch (bus)
cycle
get up
go home
go to bed
have got
lie (down)
listen to
look after
look at
paint
rain
sleep
snow
stand (up)
talk to
think
visit

awful
beautiful
cold
hot
terrible
warm

already
a lot
at the weekend
at work
even
only
every (day)
other (s)

across
along
on (+ days of week)
outside
under

then

Days of the week

Unit 8
bathroom
bedroom
country (opp town)
door
fish
floor (first)
garden
ground (floor)
hall
holiday
journey
kitchen
meat
minute
month
river

sitting room
sort
stairs
study
toilet
underground
vegetable
window
year

eat
get (to work)
look (it looks . . .)
take (a taxi)
take (+ time)
travel

blue
brown
cheap
different
easy
first
green
hungry
lazy
lucky
next
red
second
third
thirsty
top
yellow

abroad
altogether
always
ever

far
never
often
on (holiday)
once
sometimes
three times
twice
usually

another
each

How far?
How long?
How often?

Cheers!
Happy birthday!
What about you?

Unit 9
assistant
autumn
bag
card
club
date
end
factory
library
meal
message
perfume
play (theatre)
spring
station
summer

sweater
term
T-shirt
watch
winter

dance
drink
enjoy
give
happen
know (a place)
let's (+ verb)
look forward to
need
say
tell

boring
exciting
expensive
fast
free (opp busy)
fresh (air)
long (time)
loud
own
sad
slow
tired

back (I'll phone . . .)
not . . . either
on (It's on at . . .)
too (+ adjective)

anything
something
nothing

in (+ months, seasons)
on (+ dates)

Which?
Why?
Why not?

because

How nice!
I'm afraid
See you then.
Speaking.

Months of the year
Ordinal numbers
  (1st, 2nd, 3rd etc)

Unit 11
airport
cash
cheque
coach
coat
clothes
dinner
dress
fortnight
handbag
jeans
lunchtime
medium
mountain
rest (of the time)
shirt
size
skirt
tour

trip
trousers

bring
cost
have a look at
learn
pay
stay
suit (v)
try (on)

large
marvellous
pleased
pretty
smart
tight

a bit
tomorrow

everything

Can I help you?
Have a nice time.
Here you are.
It suits you.
That's a good idea.
Yes, certainly.
Yes, of course.

Unit 12
answer
car park
game
hair
hand
homework
lift
nightclub
notebook
paper
person
question
relative
road
sea (side)
word

borrow
brush
choose
count
drop
find
help
hit
keep
lose
mind
pick up
run
stop
touch
wash
win

dangerous
difficult
great (=marvellous)
ill
main
quiet
short
special
wet

also
clearly
down
else
loudly
more
so (near)
quietly
wrong

each
everyone
everywhere
someone

out of

Don't worry!
Never mind!
Oh dear!
That's very kind of you.

Unit 13
boyfriend
carton
colleague
corner
cream
detective
group
luggage
neighbour
police
trouble
university

be missing
break
break into
clear up
come from
cut
find out
get married
go out with (somebody)
hope
know (somebody)
marry
post
put
repair
show
shut
spend (time, money)
steal
take
take away
wait
wear

embarrassed
favourite
hard
shy
surprised

alone
perhaps (not)

between
into

anyone
no one

Can you do me a favour?
Is anything wrong?
Just one moment.
Oh no!
What else?
What's the matter?

Unit 14
ball
bottle
camp
education
examination
experience
goal
glove
interpreter
label
menu
rollerskate
running shoes
shorts
shower
sports bag
star
strap
stripe
success
suitcase
thing

catch (a ball)
change
cry
hear from (somebody)
invite
jump
make (bed)
order
sound (It sounds . . .)
tidy
wash up

gold
important
outdoor
political
romantic
safe
silver
topical
true

luckily
yet

Whose?

Congratulations!
Good luck!
I quite like . . .
It's time to go.
Take care of yourselves.

Language form/focus

Unit 1 Arrival

Present simple tense: verb *be* (singular) – positive, negative
    and interrogative
Personal pronouns: *I, you, it*
Question word: *What?*
Possessive adjectives: *my, your, his, her*
Good morning/afternoon/evening.
Mr, Mrs, Miss, Ms
Numbers: 0-10
Preposition: *in*
Conjunctions: *and, or*
Please + verb; *Here's your* + noun

Unit 2 Pleased to meet you

Hello. How do you do.
Demonstrative pronoun: *this*
Present simple tense: verb *be* (singular and plural)
Verb *be* + nationality adjective
Question word: *Where?*
Verb *be* + preposition: *from* + country
Pronouns: *he, she, we, you* (plural), *they*
Definite article: *the*
Demonstrative pronouns: *this, that*
Indefinite articles: *a, an*
It's/He's + adjective; *It's/It isn't* + *very* + adjective;
    It's a/an + adjective + noun
Adverbs: *here, there*
Adjectives: *big, small, good, new, nice*
Quantifier: *all*

Unit 3 I like London

Question word: *How? (How are you?)*
Very + adverbs: *well, fine*
Present simple tense: verb *like* (singular)
    –positive, negative and interrogative with auxiliary
    verb: *do/does*
Plural of nouns (regular and irregular)
Conjunction: *but*
Very + adverb: *much*
Present simple tense: verb *live* (singular and plural) –positive,
    negative and interrogative
Prepositions of place: *in, on*
Definite article: *the*
Present simple tense: verbs *do, work, study*
Genitive singular ending *'s*
Question word: *How? (How do you spell . . .?)*
Letters of the alphabet A-Z

Unit 4 Coffee or tea?

Present simple tense: *want a piece/cup/glass of/a packet of . . .*
Question word: *How much?*
Numbers 10 – 1,000,000
Modal verb: *can* (request)
Demonstrative adjectives: *this, that, these, those*
Gerund (*-ing* form) after verbs: *like, hate, love*
Inversion with auxiliary verb: *do (So do I./Nor do I.)*
Question word: *Who?*
Object pronouns: *him, her* etc
Modal verb: *can* (ability) – positive, negative and interrogative
Question word: *How old? She's/he's five. It's ten years old.*
Sorry!
That's all right.

Unit 6 Getting around

Past simple tense: verb *be* (singular and plural) – positive,
    negative and interrogative
Past time adverbials: *yesterday, this morning* etc
Preposition of place: *at*
It was + adjective
Want to + verbs *buy, get, go to*
Countable and uncountable nouns with *a, an, some*
Genitive ending *'s* with shops
There is (There's) . . . Is there . . .?
Prepositions of place: *near, next to, opposite, on*
Modal verb: *can* (possibility)
Indefinite pronoun: *one*
Imperative (infinitive without *to*): verb *turn*
Adverbs: *left, right*
Clock times: full, half, quarter hours + five minute intervals
Prepositions of time: *to, past*
Present simple tense: verbs *open, close, leave, arrive, start,*
    finish – positive and interrogative
Time adverbials: *in the morning/afternoon* etc
Preposition of time: *at*
Question words: *When?/What time?*
Quantifiers: *some, many, most*
Prepositions of time: *after, before, until*

Unit 7 Sunday in the park

Present continuous tense – positive, negative and interrogative
Present simple tense: verbs of daily routine
Time adverbials: *every* + *day/morning* etc; *at the weekend*
Gerund (*-ing* form) after verb *go*
Prepositions of time: *after, before, on*
Zero article, eg *go to work/school/church*
Days of the week
Have got – positive, negative and interrogative
Any in interrogative and negative sentences
Possessive adjectives: *our, their*
It's + *quite/very* + adjective
Exclamations with *Isn't it . . .!*